T0147327

THE STRONG'S

Constance Kinney

authorHOUSE®

AuthorHouse™
1663 Liberty Drive
Bloomington, IN 47403
www.authorhouse.com
Phone: 1-800-839-8640

First published by AuthorHouse 4/12/2011

ISBN: 978-1-4567-6392-3 (sc)
ISBN: 978-1-4567-6391-6 (dj)
ISBN: 978-1-4567-6390-9 (e)

Library of Congress Control Number: 2011905870

Printed in the United States of America

THE STRONG'S

At one time or another, as creatures of creation, we will all face a storm. The storm may be rocky, or it may be smooth. It is up to us as beings of existence to recognize when a storm is approaching. We all deal with our storms in our own personal manners of difference.

The Strong's, is a story of a family who faced many storms. No matter how great, their faith remarkably carried them through each and every storm. Walking into a storm blindsided, indubitably causes destruction, pain, and even death. As with any other challenge, preparation is the key in overcoming unbearable situations.

We must ask ourselves, if a mighty and great storm came into our lives today, would we be able to weather it?

The Trespasser

The naked, mutilated, and mangled body of Ruth Strong lay there on the creek's edge. Ruth's bare body was not just exposed to the elements of her surroundings, but also to any eye that could see.

Her breathe had been stolen, her soul had been violated, by a monstrous trespasser; a trespasser, who felt as if something as simple as covering her nakedness, would have stalled his flee to escape his horrific sin.

Who, what, how, could any being have such hatred in their heart to have done something this horrendous to another being! Trespassers flee. They flee to avoid the conviction of their sins.

All who may have fled from the conviction of man have not escaped the conviction of the Lord.

Chapter One

His head was throbbing with the word,
DEAD pounding against his skull.

Kentucky, 1920s …

It was a bitter and chilly day for 17 year old Jeremiah Strong. The sun had just set and the temperature was quickly dropping. Jeremiah was wrapped as tight as he could get. Before leaving for work, earlier that morning, Jeremiah's mother Ruth made sure that her son wouldn't get frost bite while out working the fields. Every morning before Jeremiah would go off to work, Ruth always prepared for Jeremiah, what he would need for the day. So today wasn't any different.

After working a long treacherous day in the fields, Jeremiah was looking forward to going home. He anxiously anticipated the aroma of stew in the air and the warmness coming from the heater in his home. Actually arriving home was Jeremiah's high point of any day.

As Jeremiah, Harold, Ronnie, and Kent were walking down the trail leading out of the fields, he noticed people running rapidly towards them. The young men didn't know what to make of this. As the people running towards them got closer, Jeremiah noticed who he thought was his cousin Wilton. To his amazement, it was Wilton. He was running so fast that he tripped and fell at Jeremiah's feet. Jeremiah reached down to help Wilton to his feet.

Wilton started rambling so, that Jeremiah had to shake him to get

1

him to calm down. Jeremiah quickly helped Wilton compose himself. Looking at his cousin with an inquisitive eye, Jeremiah asked, "Wilton, what's got you so upset." Wilton still in distress over his news, responded, "Jay, its Tee Ruth!"

"What about Momma, what is it!" asked Jeremiah strongly.

Wilton, with most of the energy ablated from his body, slowly began to tell Jeremiah what the elders had told him about Ruth. Although he dreaded telling Jeremiah, Wilton knew that the news would be better coming from him, other than anyone else.

"LeCester and Marvin, was going down to the bottoms to do some hunting and they seen Tee Ruth laying half way in the creek. She didn't have any clothes on and she was beat up pretty bad," responded Wilton.

Jeremiah heard the words Wilton had spoken, but at the same time, he didn't comprehend what Wilton's words actually meant. With a calming presence, Jeremiah asked, "Wilton, please slow down and tell me what you just said, again."

Wilton repeated the same words to Jeremiah, only slower. "Jay, Tee Ruth is dead; they found her body in the creek down by the bottoms. Come with us, everybody down at the bottoms wanted us to come and get you," said Wilton.

As Jeremiah blankly stared at Wilton's lips moving, his body was anesthetized, with distress. All of a sudden, everything went desensitized around Jeremiah. At this moment, he lost all mental understanding of reality. He was ignorant of all Wilton had said. He no longer saw Wilton, or anyone else next to him. His head was throbbing with the word, DEAD pounding against his skull. Subconsciously, Jeremiah was taken aback. He battled with insane thoughts contemplating within his head: *'Momma is dead … no Momma is at home waiting on me … no no no, my Momma is dead'* …

Wilton and the other three boys that were with them, had to physically carry Jeremiah to the church. After arriving, Wilton, Harold, Ronnie, and Kent were instructed by an elderly woman from their town, to keep Jeremiah outside until they had finished preparing Ruth's body for burial. The four young men did as much as they could to try and comfort Jeremiah. All of their efforts where going unheard, for the news Jeremiah had just heard had an abducted his state of being. Realizing that their efforts where unheard, the four young men left him to grieve alone.

There were six women from the town that took on the intricate task of preparing Ruth's body. The oldest of the six, Brenda, covered everything in the church that had a reflection. This was a custom that had been practiced in their culture for many years. Being the oldest of all the women, according to their custom, Brenda had to lead in the preparation of cleaning the deceased. Being such a strong faith filled woman, helped Brenda when it came to matters such as this.

The women were good friends with Ruth, and knew what she would have wanted. Brenda chose a beautiful purple dress for Ruth to be laid to rest in. All the women went into the backroom of the church where the body had been laid. They had gathered all the materials they would need to clean Ruth's body.

Brenda then crouched down next to the table. Next to her was a washbasin full of hot water and lye soap. She had brought with her two white clothes. She took one and soaked it in the hot water. Then she began to clean Ruth from her face, down to her feet.

As Brenda continued cleaning Ruth's body, one of the other women began to quietly sing, "*Swing low, sweet chariot, coming for to carry me home, swing low, sweet chariot, coming for to carry me home, If you get there before I do, coming for to carry me home, tell all my friends, I'm coming too, coming for to carry me home*" ... ... The women continued to sing and hum as they cleaned Ruth's body.

The sight of Ruth's body was deleterious to any eye that rested upon it. Her face and head had been beaten so badly, that as Brenda wiped, portions of her skull and face were coming off onto the cloth. It became so overbearing, that Brenda had to stop wiping and ask God for the strength to continue cleansing Ruth's body.   Seeing this was atrocious for the women to absorb, but they all knew that they had to continue. By the time they had finished, they had gone through eight washbasins of hot water. Brenda thought to herself, how anyone could do this to another human being, especially a woman. She couldn't think of anyone in their community who could be responsible for doing this to Ruth. After the body was completely cleaned, they dressed Ruth.

They had did the best they could do to Ruth's body, in order for Jeremiah to view it before the wake. The six women kneeled around Ruth's bed, bowed their heads and began to pray. Since Brenda was the oldest of the women, she led the prayer. The women prayed for over two hours. After they finished praying, Brenda blessed the body and left the room to go obtain Jeremiah. The other women sheltered the body with a large piece of white cloth.

Reality slowly surfaced to Jeremiah's surroundings. The next time his eyes were opened, Jeremiah realized that he was sitting on tree stump next to the church. By now, his eyes were distended and he had omnipotent pains in his head. He had barely enough strength to raise his head to see Brenda standing next to him. She reached out as to help lift him to his feet.

"Jeremiah, it's time for you to go in and say goodbye to your Momma," said Brenda. Jeremiah knew that this moment was coming, but he had not prepared himself physically or mentally to deal with it. With Brenda's help, Jeremiah unhurriedly arose to his feet.

As Brenda stalwartly clutched Jeremiah beneath his under arm, carrying him inside, she knew that this was going to be difficult for him to bear. She offered him as much strength as she had within herself, for his physical and mental state of being. As the two got closer to the back door of the church, angst was rapidly setting in for Jeremiah. He knew on the other side of the door, was the inert body of his Mother. Although he knew his mother was on the other side of the door, veracity assured him that she wasn't alive.

Walking towards the backroom, Jeremiah felt, for every one bodily step that he took forward, he psychologically felt that he was taking two steps backwards. The short distance from the side of the church to the backroom appeared to be perpetual to Jeremiah. As Brenda along with Jeremiah, stood at the door to the backroom, he regrettably pushed the door opened.

"Do you need me to go in with you?" asks Brenda. Holding her hands with a burly clasp, Jeremiah replied, "No mam, I want to go in alone."

Brenda freed herself from Jeremiah's clasp, lovingly kissed his forehead and eased him into the room. She then closed the door behind her and joined the other women in another room in the church to continue praying for Ruth's soul and Jeremiah strength.

As Jeremiah stood there looking across the room at his mother's body covered with a white cloth, numerous thoughts were clouding his inevitable breakdown: *'why Momma … why me … why now … how did this happen ... who did this ... what am I to do without her'* ... With his many thoughts, roaring within his head, Jeremiah took the obligatory steps to reach his mother. Once there, he knew he had to pull the cloth back. With ambiguous vision, because of his many tears, Jeremiah fell to the floor next to his mother's body.

Jeremiah's breath was coming and going. He felt as if he had a lump in his throat that was making it hard for him to breath. With one hand, he grasped his own throat to try and lessen the lump. With his entire body trembling, he used his other hand to pull back the cloth from his mother's body. He didn't know what to expect once the cloth had been removed. Gradually pulling the cloth away from his mother, he began to see her hair, then her forehead, then her eyes, then her nose, then her mouth. As his eyes traveled further down her body, he noticed her necklace wasn't around her neck.

Jeremiah knew that the necklace was of great significance to Ruth, because it was the first thing his father had given her. It was given to him by his mother. It was an old Indian necklace that had R.S. carved in one of the stones and Ruth didn't go anywhere without. He figured whomever had done this to his mother must have taken it.

'Who is this, this can't be Momma', he thought to himself. As Jeremiah intensely gazed at what he felt **LIFE** had given him, his grieve became rage. As he sat there next to his mother's lifeless body, pondering his emotions, he wanted someone to pay for what had happened to his mother.

With anger, hate, and frustration in his heart, Jeremiah laid his head on his mother's chest and openly started talking to her. "Momma don't worry, I'll get whoever did this to you. I don't care what I have to do; somebody is going to pay for this. I'm so sorry I wasn't there to protect you", said Jeremiah.

His emotions were all over the place. He went from rage to sorrow. "I knew I should have come straight home after I left the fields. No, I had to listen to Michael and go see some girls. Momma please come back, please Momma, I need you. I don't want to live here without you. I swear I'll do better. I will make sure not to stay out late, if you just come back," Jeremiah pleaded.

To Jeremiah, his pleas were inaudible. Death was fairly new to him. So he didn't quite understand the actuality of it all. The only other deceased people he knew where his father Seth and his Uncle Joe. Joe was Ruth's only brother, and Wilton's father. At the time of Seth's death, Jeremiah was too young to grasp the concept of his father's death. All he understood and slowly accepted was that his father was not coming home. After the death of Joe, Ruth did her best to explain death to Jeremiah yet again. As far as Ruth knew, Jeremiah handled both deaths as well as to be expected.

While there at his mother's side, Jeremiah recalled what she had told him about death, when his Uncle Joe died. After reflecting on her words, Jeremiah realized that people are born, and then they die. Because of his mother, Jeremiah did know that she trusted in God to not only carry her through the loss of her husband and brother, but she also would tell him daily, 'Jeremiah, we have to trust in God for all things.' At this very moment, he didn't identify with her words, but as he grew older, he would.

Jeremiah slowly began to gather his thoughts and control his feelings. He rose from where he knelt, and reached over and kissed his mother on the lips. As he did this, he looked at her with every fiber of love he held, for he knew this would be the last time he would see her face. Afterwards, he pulled the white cloth back over his mother's face and kneeled back down to pray.

The only knowledge of prayer Jeremiah had is what he received from his mother. Although he didn't understand why his mother would always pray, read the bible, or talk to God, he knew that it had to be right, because his mother did it. Anything revolving around God meant a lot to her, so they began to mean a lot to him.

Jeremiah bowed his head, and began to pray, *"God, I don't know why you chose to take my Momma, I'm not going to even question you about that, because she would get mad if I did. She told me that everyone must die one day. I guess today was her day to die. God, I don't know what will happen tomorrow, or any of the days after, but I am asking you to please guide me, for I know not the way to go. I'm on bending knees asking you to keep Momma and keep me. God I pray that you will bless me with the same strength and faith in you, that you blessed Momma with. God, I am lost and I am alone. I need you God. I need you in every way and in everything that I do. God, every time Momma would end a prayer, she would always say, "Lord God, I pray for all these things in your son Jesus name". So God, I would like to do the same thing. Before I do, may you be blessed, may*

Momma be blessed, and may I be blessed. In your son Jesus name, I pray for all these things. Amen." said Jeremiah.

After praying, Jeremiah was able to physically compose himself. Inside he felt as if the lump was gone, he was able to breathe freely, and the immensity he had felt on his chest, was gone. He stood and looked down at his mother laying there. He knew his reality: He knew his mother was gone, he knew that she wasn't coming back, he knew from this day forward, that in order for him to make it through, that he would have to trust in God, just as his mother did.

He bent down again, pulling the cloth to cover her face, Jeremiah kissed his mother one last time, and said, good-bye. Jeremiah left from the presence of his mother and went into the next room. He was met by Brenda.

"She's ready Mrs. Brenda," said Jeremiah. "Okay baby, are you sure?" asked Brenda.

"Yes mam, let them go ahead before I lose my nerve," replied Jeremiah. He left from the church and went for a walk. He knew what the elder men had to do.

Brenda motioned for the elder men to come inside and place Ruth's body into casket. The casket had been made immediately by the men, after Ruth's body was found. Once inside, the men carefully placed Ruth into the casket. Brenda came in and laid the white cloth over Ruth and the top to the casket was put in place. Ruth's casket was then taken and placed in the front of the church.

Everyone that lived within this small community came and gathered together to view the body. Because of the arduous damage to Ruth's face, the lid was not taken of the casket, as a sign of respect. Isaiah Carr, the oldest man there, spoke the final words over Ruth's remains.

He spoke of who she was in life, her benevolence, her giving heart, and the love she openly shared with God, Jeremiah, nephew Wilton, and her neighbors. Ruth's death took an extreme toll on many of the lives present at her wake. She was commonly referred as," Momma Ruth"; not only because she was the oldest woman in the town, but she also had such a nurturing spirit. It was obvious by the amount of people present at the wake, that Ruth was greatly respected and loved.

After Isaiah finished his dedication to Ruth, the casket was closed. Isaiah, along with Brenda, blessed Ruth's remains. Eight of the strongest men present, stoutly clutched a section of the casket and carried it from the church. The men carrying the casket lead the way to the final resting place for Ruth. As the men carried the casket, they were followed by, what seemed like, the entire town.

Her casket was buried next to her late husband and her brother, who both preceded her in death. After the casket had been covered by dirt, onlookers placed single wild flowers around Ruth's grave.

Jeremiah didn't attend the wake or the burial. He had already said his final good-bye to his mother. At the time of the wake, Jeremiah had left and wondered off to be alone. The solitude was exactly what he needed at the time. He sat and contemplated his thoughts about the future. Although his best friend was gone, he knew that he had to continue on with life. He felt that he now needed to strive even harder to make his mother and father proud.

Jeremiah's father, Seth, had passed on when Jeremiah was only two years old, from heart failure. From early childhood until her untimely death, Ruth instilled in Jeremiah the values that Seth wanted him to have. Even with absent memories, Jeremiah was similar to his father in so many ways. Ruth would often tell Jeremiah, that he was just like his father. This was very well taken by Jeremiah.

As Jeremiah sat there alone, he could hear the faint sounds of everyone who had attended the wake and burial. There were laughs and also tears, reflections of the impact that Ruth had left. Jeremiah was pleased with the amount of affection everyone showed concerning his well being.

As the long day slowly turned to darkness, Jeremiah had thoughts of compunction; he knew that he had to return home. He stood up from where he sat, dusted himself off, and began the dreadful walk home. While ambling home, he took the time to admire and appreciate things that he had never noticed. He saw the stars with new eyes, the moon had never been so brilliant, the night air had never smelled so new, his footsteps had never had purpose, and the presence of life felt meaningful.

Once inside his home, Jeremiah decided to go into his mother's room and hold any of her things that reminded him of her presence. He gathered all her dresses from a chest of drawers, and laid them on the bed. He sat there contemplating on what to do with his mom's things. He came to the conclusion to give Ruth's dresses to Mrs. Brenda. He knew that she would know who needed the dresses the most. Jeremiah knew that giving the dresses to someone in need would be what his mother would have wanted. He gathered all the dresses to take them into the other room to wash them before giving them to Mrs. Brenda the next day.

Jeremiah and his mother didn't own many material possessions, but what they did own, was treated as though it were priceless. Ruth would always minister to Jeremiah the importance of gratefulness of all things that God saw fit for them to have. Jeremiah, being a humble person, always did what his mother taught him.

Jeremiah placed a large pot of water onto the wood burning heater. After the water came to an aggressive boil, he put into the pot a small amount of lye soap, to cleanse the dresses.

While the dresses were boiling clean, Jeremiah sat there intensely gazing at the steam evaporating from the pot. The silence in the house as he sat there alone was brutally painful. He went back into the room and stripped the bed coverings from the bed and carried them back into the next room. He cradled the coverings as to inexhaustibly hold on to his mother's presence. As he sat there, he was able to hear every thought, good and bad, meandering through his mind. The thoughts of confronting tomorrow began to overcrowd all other thoughts.

Jeremiah began to concentrate on the roaring sound of the boiling water. His eyes then began to weigh heavy. His emotions and thoughts had put a strain on his mental state, which sequentially caused strain on his body. The wear and tear of all that Jeremiah had gone through on this day, caused Jeremiah's eyes to finally shut, and his head dropped to his chest.

While Jeremiah sat there sound asleep in the chair next to the warm wood heater, the feeling of someone embracing his face, startled him into waking up. He slowly opened his eyes, while at the same time, raising his head from where it was resting upon his chest. He then saw a vague figure kneeling next to him. Perplexed, he used his hands to clear the sleepiness from his eyes. He took a second, clearer look, at the figure kneeling next to him.

Jeremiah's mouth dropped open and his body went paralyzed. Although excited, over what he thought he was seeing, his body was numb to his immediate surroundings. The thought, *'this can't be, momma was buried today'*, quickly entered in and left his mind. He then realized that he was undoubtedly looking at his mother kneeling next to him.

Jeremiah found enough courage to finally speak. "Momma is this you?" he asked.

The figure that appeared to be Ruth, to Jeremiah, responded, "Yes baby, it's me, Momma. I came to say good-bye."

Nearly in a state of perpetual disbelief, Jeremiah's physical physic started trembling with desperation. Jeremiah starts to speak, "but, Momma how did you … Just as the next word was departing his mouth, he felt his mother's finger pressing against his lips, preventing him from speaking. He didn't resist, he didn't continue speaking.

In a soft, almost serene voice, Jeremiah heard his mother's voice, yet again, saying, "Shhhh, quiet now. We don't have a lot of time. Let me speak. I need you to look underneath the bottom of the lower chest of drawers in my room. There you will find a wooden box. Inside the box, you will find my Holy Bible. I need you to take that bible and keep it with you. I need you to read it, meditate in it, day and night, as if you where trying to figure out a puzzle. One day you will understand the importance of why I'm telling you to do this."

She went on to say, "Please don't have any doubt concerning our circumstances. I've always told you that God has a reason for everything that he does. It is important to me that you trust that God has a reason for my passing on. It is not my place, nor yours, to question the reason. From this point on, put your trust in no earthly human. Only trust God, for he will see you through this storm and all the storms you will face. Do not think that you need your cousin Wilton for anything, for he is a man of this earth. God, will comfort you, in your time of need; as long as you do as I have asked of you, READ AND MEDITATE IN GOD'S WORD, DAY AND NIGHT! Baby, take heed to my words, for they are not in vain, but instead, love. I must go now, but always remember, that the love I have for you on this day, will always be in your heart. This love can't be taken by any man. I love you, Jeremiah Strong."

Jeremiah sat there still stupefied with fear and excitement, but he was ecstatic over seeing his mother, hearing his mother's voice, and inhaling the comforting aroma of his mother's presence. He felt a physically powerful, freezing breeze against his face! He instantaneously closed and reopened his eyes. He leaped from the chair, in search of his mother. He stopped where he stood.

Rambling aloud, he says, "Okay, what's going on? God, what is wrong with me? Am I losing my mind?"

For a brief second, Jeremiah assumed that he had to have been dreaming. This thought was overpowered by what Jeremiah knew to be true, his mother was there. Being ignorant to this type of encounter, Jeremiah wondered how this could be. He then remembered something that his mother had just spoken to him, not to question anything that God does. Jeremiah obediently accepted seeing his mother on this night, which was the night after she was laid to rest.

After Jeremiah made a conscious decision to accept speaking with his mother, he proceeded to do as she had asked. Although he remained physically shaken by this occurrence, Jeremiah was able to gather his composure and go into his mother's bedroom.

Once inside the room, Jeremiah crooked down and pulled the drawer all the way out. He laid the drawer next to him on the floor. He then reached inside the hollow space, which had held the drawer. He felt it! A nervous, yet uneasy, Jeremiah proceeded to grab a tight hold to the box.

Jeremiah sat there for a brief second, staring at the box. He then slowly lifted the lid off the box. To his amazement, the first thing he saw was the Holy Bible. He started to realize that he wasn't going crazy, and that the figure was actually his mother. Before this night, Jeremiah never knew where his mother kept her Holy Bible. The bible was in the exact place that his mother said it would be.

The bible wasn't the only thing in the box. Jeremiah also retrieved a photo, with his mom in a beautiful dress and his father standing behind her with both his hands resting on her shoulders. He had never seen this photo. Seeing the photo only added to his sorrow, but at the same time, powerfully fueling his much needed comfort. Seeing his father on the photo took Jeremiah back to a more satisfying time in his life. It had been many years since he had seen an image of his father. Lying underneath the photo was 77 dollars. Jeremiah placed the photo inside the bible, while leaving the money in the box.

He dawdled into the front room. He laid the bible down in the chair so he could tend to the bed coverings. The water had nearly evaporated from the pot. Jeremiah took the bed coverings from the pot and hung them outside on the clothes line. He took advantage of this opportunity of unwanted silence and opened the bible, to begin reading.

Aloud, he spoke, "Well God, what better place to begin than the beginning. God, I ask that you bless me with the understanding and the knowledge of your words in this holy bible. I pray that you will continue to fill me with your words and your truth. God, I pray for these things in your son Jesus' name. Amen."

Jeremiah couldn't explain the feeling he was experiencing at this very moment, but it was an invincible feeling. Circumspectly he began to read, "In the beginning, God created the heavens and the earth," … … The next morning when Jeremiah awoke, he noticed that he had read the entire first three books of the bible and had begun on the fourth. This day was the beginning of Jeremiah's new journey; a journey that he would not be taking alone, for now he had found his place with God.

Chapter Two

Over the past three years, over four counties, the
bodies of seven colored women, including Ruth Strong,
and one 13 year old girl, have been found.

The E.R.O.C.P …

JEREMIAH ROSE, GOT DRESSED and he prepared some lunch for work that day. He placed his bible in the sack containing his lunch. He wanted to do as his mother had spoken to him, so he carried the bible to read whenever he received a break. As he was heading out the door, he grabbed the bigger sack holding his mother's clothes and left the house.

While walking towards Mrs. Brenda's house (to give her the clothes) Jeremiah anticipated telling his cousin Wilton about what he had experienced the night before.

Wilton and Jeremiah had been close every since Joe, Wilton's father, had died. After his death, Wilton's mom had a nervous breakdown. She had been said to have left to go live with family. When he lost both his dad and his mom, Wilton was taken in by his Aunt Ruth when he was 13. Ruth was not unfamiliar with death; therefore, she was able to help her nephew cope with his lose. She loved him, for he was the seed of her only brother.

At first, Ruth felt that having Wilton living and working with Jeremiah would be good for the both of them. Ruth did all she could for Wilton, but it didn't seem to be enough. After the loss of his parents,

Wilton didn't appear to take an interest in anything that was meaningful. Although his behavior concerning obedience and learning displeased Ruth, she continued to support him, even as an adult. Whenever doing anything for Jeremiah, Ruth would always show consideration towards Wilton. Even with a five year age difference between the two boys, they maintained a close bond. Having this bond, only added to excitement Jeremiah had held within, to share his experience with his cousin.

Jeremiah approached Mrs. Brenda's house. She was standing out front with some neighbors. Something had caught their attention up the street, because everyone's attention was looking in that direction.

Jeremiah greeted Mrs. Brenda and the neighbors, "good morning everybody."

"Good morning to you Jeremiah," everyone responded.

Walking up into the midst of the small crowd, Jeremiah hands the sack to Brenda. "Mrs. Brenda, these are my mother's clothes, I thought that she would want you to have them," he says. Brenda reaches and takes the bag, while giving Jeremiah an embrace of gratitude. While hugging him, Brenda says, "thank you for these things Jeremiah. I know this was a hard thing to do, but these things will be a blessing to someone who really needs them."

Brenda steps back and looks sincerely into Jeremiah's eyes, and says, "You have the same giving spirit as Ruth had; I know you will be okay."

One of the neighbors, strongly stated, "Here they come." Jeremiah, along with everyone else standing in the yard, glanced up the way to see two men approaching. It was almost never that strangers visited their small town; therefore, seeing these two men entering the town put curiosity in the hearts of the towns' people.

Both men were black and wore black suits with brims on. They appeared to be distinguished and looking for something or someone. As the two men stood before the crowd of locals, they both removed their brims, held it with one hand, bringing it down and placing it on their chests.

The taller of the two men spoke first, "Good day folks. My name is Johnny Rae and this here is my partner, Larry Spence. We're from a couple counties up the road. We're here on behalf of an organization called, E.R.O.C.P, Equal Rights of Colored People. We came here to look into the murder of a local woman here, by the name of Ruth

Strong. We have reason to believe that her murder was not just a random thing," said Johnny Rae.

Hearing this, took everyone by surprise, especially Jeremiah. He had assumed, like any other crime committed in their town, his mother's death wouldn't be investigated. There was no governmental structure in their town. Black people living in this area had to solely rely on justice from the sheriff over the entire county, whom was a white man. The only time the people of this town ever saw the sheriff, was if a crime, was said to have been committed, to any white person by a black person, in the "white part" of the county. Hearing that an organization existed that sincerely cared for the well being and justice being served for black people was pleasing to the entire crowd of people.

Larry Spence took over Johnny's conversation, and said, "Although we don't have the power to arrest anyone, we gather evidence and information involving crimes against colored people. We then pass any evidence and or information gathered to the sheriff of the county. If the evidence is proven to be accurate, an arrest is made. When our organization received word that a colored woman was found naked and beaten to death, we were sent here."

Johnny Rae started to speak again, "Over the past three years, over four counties, the bodies of seven colored women, including Ruth Strong, and one 13 year old girl, have been found. We have gathered a lot of evidence and we strongly feel that we are getting close to finding out who is responsible for these murders. We need to talk to anyone who has any information about Ruth's murder. The first person or persons we need to speak to is whoever found her body."

Isaiah stepped up to Johnny Rae and Larry and reached out to shake their hands. While shaking their hands, Isaiah spoke, "Hello Mr. Johnny, Mr. Larry, and good day to the both of you. My name is Isaiah Carr; I'm the pastor and the eldest of this here little town. All of us here want to know what devil did this to Sister Ruth. We all love her. We will do whatever needs to be done to help you folks find him."

Isaiah thought that it would be better if the men were able to have some privacy when they questioned people. Since they were all gathered in the front of Brenda's house, he asked her if they could do the questioning inside her house. She agreed. Isaiah then said to Johnny and Larry, "Mrs. Brenda here is going to be neighborly enough to let you use her house to question any of us that you need to."

Brenda and Isaiah showed the men inside. Once inside the house, Brenda said, "You gentlemen have a seat there on the couch next to the heater and I will go and put on some water for coffee.

"I figure you gentlemen might won't to talk to Marvin and LeCester Hill first, they the ones who found the body," said Isaiah.

"Yes Pastor, we would. Can you get them for us," asked Larry. Isaiah went outside to get the two brothers.

When Isaiah made it outside, he beckoned for the two to come inside. "All you boys have to do is tell the men what happened and what you saw when you found Sister Ruth." said Isaiah. He then led Marvin and LeCester inside to where the men sat on the couch.

As Isaiah, Marvin, and LeCester walked inside, Jeremiah as well as everyone else wondered who was next to go in. Jeremiah never knew the entire details surrounding the men finding Ruth, so he wanted to know if he could sit in and listen to everyone that would be questioned. He walked up and opened the door to see Johnny and Larry sitting next to each other on the couch and Marvin and LeCester facing them. Isaiah was standing next to the front door.

"Excuse me gentlemen, I'm sorry for interrupting. My name is Jeremiah Strong, I'm Ruth's son. I would be much obliged if you would allow me to sit in on the questioning," said Jeremiah.

"Yea son, come in and sit next to me here on the couch," said Johnny Rae.

Before Jeremiah starts to walk over to the couch, Isaiah gently grabs his arm, and asked, "Are you sure that you want to hear this Jeremiah?"

"Yes sir, I want to know who, what, and how this happened to my momma," Jeremiah responded. Isaiah then reluctantly released Jeremiah's arm and he went and sat on the couch next to Johnny and Larry.

Johnny reached inside a case that he was carrying and pulled out two writing pads. He kept one and handed the other one to Larry. These pads were used to document any information they gathered from their questioning. They both placed their pencils on their pads. "Okay, which one of you wants to start first?" asked Johnny.

LeCester then leads the conversation. "Pleased to meet you both, my name is LeCester Hill and this here is my younger brother, Marvin Hill. Well I and Marvin got a late start on hunting, so we took a short cut down through the Bottoms, to make up for starting off so late. Far off we saw somebody running into the thickets close by the creek. I couldn't make out who it was, but Marvin here, said it kind of looked like Joe's boy, Wilton. We didn't pay it much mind and kept on walking. As we got a little closer to the creek, I started to see something lying on the ground. You know how it is when you see something out of place? I thought maybe somebody had killed a deer and left it on the ground," said LeCester.

Marvin then nervously took over, and said, "When we made it to what we thought was a deer, that's when we seen, it wasn't a deer, it was what was left of Sister Ruth. Ces started throwing up and got weak in the knees and fell to the ground. I, myself, almost passed out because of how bad her face looked. It was all smashed in and bloody. It looked like something wild had got a hold of her. I took my coat off and laid it on her, because she didn't have a lick of clothes on."

As the two were recalling what they had seen and done, Jeremiah sat there in disbelief. The tears couldn't stop flowing. He began to get nauseated. Larry noticed Jeremiah's obvious pain, and asked, "Do you want to continue listening? If this is too much, you should step outside until we finish," said Larry.

"No sir, let them go on. I'll be okay, its tuff, but I need to know what happened to my momma," Jeremiah responded.

Johnny Rae motioned for the two to continue speaking. LeCester continued to speak, "it was a big rock soaked in blood, next to her head. I asked Marvin, who in the hell did this? He just said, Ces, I don't know, but we got to go tell Pastor Isaiah; so he can tell her boy and her nephew," said LeCester.

"So I told Ces, that I will stay with Sister Ruth and he should go and get Pastor Isaiah and some of the men folk. So Ces took off. As I sat there I noticed that the coat hadn't covered Sister Ruth's entire body. Her face was left uncovered. My eyes fell on what was left of her face. I remember thinking, Jesus, who would want her to suffer like this, "said Marvin.

His emotions began to overcrowd his speech; he cleared his throat and slowly regained his composure. He began to continue with his story, "I then looked around close to where her body was laying. I was so upset; I didn't even know what I was looking for. But as I looked out across the creek, I saw something caught in some bushes. I waded out far enough to get whatever it was. It looked like it was a dress. I pulled it out of the water and laid it next to the bloody rock. The dress was all ripped and bloody, I figured it had to be Sister Ruth's dress. You know, as I was sitting there waiting on someone to come, I thought to myself, the person we seen a minute ago, couldn't have been Joe's boy, because he would have seen his auntie lying here," said Marvin.

LeCester begins to speak again, "I found Pastor Isaiah and told him everything that had happened. He told me to see if I could find Jeremiah and Wilton and he would get the other men folk gathered up. I went to Sister Ruth's house, but nobody was there, so I figured Jeremiah had already left for the fields. I knew that Wilton didn't work anywhere, so I went up to Dale Lunnie's house. I knew that he usually snuck and stayed there with Dale's daughter."

LeCester took and deep breathe and continued to speak. "Now, Dale was sitting out in the front. I asked him if Wilton was there. He said that he hoped not, but that he probably was. So he stepped in the front door and called for his daughter. She came out and he asked her if Wilton was in there with her. She said he was. Dale told her to go get Wilton. When Wilton came out, I asked him if he had been down by the creek today. He told me no, that he had been at Dale's house since last night. He asked me why I wanted to know. I told him that I and Marvin had found his Auntie Ruth's body down by the creek. He started crying and screaming at the top of his lungs, then he took off towards the creek! Me and Dale took off behind him," said LeCester.

Johnny Rae asks, "What did yall do with the dress and the rock?" Before they could respond, Isaiah spoke, "I had my wife to put it up; just in case somebody wanted later on."

"That was a very smart thing to do Pastor Isaiah. Could you get those things for us? We need to take them with us when we leave. It will be compared to other items we have collected over the course of these murders," says Larry.

Isaiah then steps out the front door and asks his Michael to go and get the box that he had put the dress and rock in. Without hesitation, Michael animatedly ran home to extract the box.

Back inside the house, Brenda had readied a pot of perking hot coffee along with fresh sweet butter rolls to serve to her visitors. The coffee and sweet butter rolls proved to be comforting to Johnny Rae and Larry. They had traveled an immense distance to investigate Ruth's murder.

Isaiah had kept items from the scene of the crime, and Johnny Rae and Larry concluded that they were very important to assisting in solving the mystery of Ruth's murder. Similar evidence had been collected in all the other unsolved murders that the E.R.O.C.P had been investigating. Johnny Rae and Larry wanted to see the body of Ruth, but they didn't receive the news of her murder until after she was already buried. The manner, in which the body was left by the trespasser, was very important in assisting with solving the case as well as seeing if Ruth's body had been mutilated in the same manner as the others.

They all sat there patiently waiting on Michael to return. As they sat there, Johnny Rae and Larry talked quietly amongst themselves. "We really need to know who that was the men saw running away," said Johnny Rae.

"As small as this town is, if that was somebody from here then one of the two would have recognized him," said Larry.

"Even with the town being small, if I had just killed somebody, I'm going to make sure that nobody sees me," said Johnny Rae.

"If who we are looking for is from here, he knows that those two men saw them. So he is either going to high tail it out of here, or he's lay low for a spell and maybe strike again," said Larry.

"I don't know Larry, if this is the same person who killed those other women why now would he kill and rape somebody Ruth Strong's age. I just don't get why he would change his pattern," said Johnny Rae.

The front door opened! Michael had returned with the box. He carefully handed the box over to Larry. "Thanks son, we have to take this with us when we leave, if that's okay," said Larry.

"Oh, yes sir, that'll be just fine. Do yall need to talk to anyone else?" asks Isaiah.

"Well a matter of fact, we would like to ask Wilton a few questions. If that was him they saw, maybe he was doing something he didn't want anyone to know about," said Johnny Rae.

Just as he said that, Jeremiah leaped to his feet! In a rage, he says, "What do you mean; doing something he didn't want anyone to know about! Wilton would never do anything to hurt Momma! For the sake of God, that's his aunt!"

Johnny Rae stood to his feet next to Jeremiah. He grabbed him by both arms and shook him. "Son, son, please calm down. We don't mean it like that. When we arrived in town this morning, before we made it to you, we stopped and talked to some more folks, trying to get information. We was told by more than one person that the "Bottoms" was a place to go if you was looking for a good time. Now, when LeCester and Marvin was telling us what happened, they said that Wilton was with a man's daughter. So I figure, if I'm looking for a good time and I don't want my old lady to know about it, I'm not talking!" replied Johnny Rae.

Jeremiah responds, "I'm sorry for getting loud. I don't mean you no disrespect, I just, I just …

"Son I know, I understand. I would be upset to in your situation. We all want the same thing. If we can just ask Wilton a few questions, we'll be on our way," said Johnny Rae.

"Could I got and get him, I need to get some fresh air anyway?" asks Jeremiah.

"Sure son, go ahead. We need to go down to the Bottoms and look around, so when you find him, just meet us down there," said Johnny Rae.

"Yes sir," replied Jeremiah. After speaking to the men Jeremiah left in search of his cousin Wilton. As he was walking down the way through the small town, visions of what LeCester and Marvin spoke of invaded his thoughts. The joy he had felt earlier this morning was slowly turning into dread. As if it were a fistfight, dread coming up with a left hook, joy doing all it could to dodge the blow! Then he remembers the words of his mother, ' Only trust God, for he will see you through this storm and all the storms you will face.' With clear thoughts and a meek grin, he says aloud, "Well dread, I guess joy knocked YOU out!"

Jeremiah continued his search for Wilton at all his usual spots. To no prevail, he couldn't find him. He headed for the Bottoms. Once there Johnny Rae and Larry were talking to a young woman that lived in the Bottoms. Jeremiah stood off until they finished talking with her.

"Hey son, did you find Wilton?' asks Johnny Rae. "No sir, I looked in the places he usually stays, but no one has seen him," replied Jeremiah.

"Well, I think we have all the information we can get. We're going to take what we gathered here and add it to what we already have on the other cases. As soon as we find out anything new, we will be contacting you. I'm going to write down our address. You feel free to write us anytime concerning your Mother's case. Don't give up, we sure wont," said Johnny Rae.

Jeremiah takes the piece of paper given to him and places it inside his bible. He then says good bye to Johnny Rae and Larry. He doesn't know what to think about why Wilton chose this moment to leave town. He realized that this is not the first time Wilton had left. Jeremiah remembered Wilton confiding in him that he sometimes got overwhelmed by losing both his parents. Leaving for a little while would always help him to clear his mind. Jeremiah just took Wilton leaving this time as maybe him losing his only aunt after losing both his parents, was too much for him to bear.

By the time the men were heading of back to where they came from, the sun was starting to set. Jeremiah looked onward as the Johnny Rae and Larry slowly drifted off into the midst of the setting sun.

Standing there in the presence of the place in which his mother had taken her last breath, Jeremiah began looking around at the scenery. He noticed what appeared to be a large stain of dried blood on the soil next to the creek. He esuriently yet demurely knew what he was looking at. He proceeded to walk over to the stain and kneeled next to it. He grabbed a hand full of the blood stained soil and let if gently fall through his fingers. Then he stood and walked out to the edge of the creek and picked up a discarded piece of a wooden plank and firmly scraped against the blood stained soil and tossed it into the creek. Once he had removed all the soil, he threw the plank into the creek as well.

Although Jeremiah had somewhat made peace with his mother's death, doing this was comforting to his quality of mind. As he stood there basking in the events of the day, he began to speak to the Lord. "My precious Father, through you I found the strength to accept Momma's death. Dear Father, I do not want the memory of the day of her death, to outweigh the memories that I have of her life. Her life meant more to me than her death. But I trust that her death is the beginning of my life with you. I will now leave this here spot, down by the creek, were momma was taken away and reassigned to a better place. I take comfort in knowing this. I will not return to this spot in all the days left of my life nor will I return here in memories. Dear God, may you be with me," said Jeremiah.

Once Jeremiah left from the spot down by the creek, he did as he said, he never returned to that spot in his life or in his memories.

Chapter Three

Well boys, it's a big move for all of us, but I wouldn't mind a change.

Jeremiah Leaves Kentucky ...

YEARS HAD GONE BY in the life of Jeremiah Strong. From a naïve 17 year old boy, he had developed into a 25 year old man. Since the death of his mother, Jeremiah had did all he could to remain strong and be the best person he could be. He did this not only for his mother but, for himself as well. He had established a reputation in his community as a hard worker and a profound follower of God. To many of the elders, he had the characteristics of both his father and mother.

Although slavery had ended in Kentucky in 1865, many Blacks felt as if it hadn't happened. There were still lynchings, inequality, segregation, and injustice amongst the Black race. There were organizations other than the E.R.O.C.P that existed in trying to make the lives of Black Americans as equal as they could. Change was slow to come in Jeremiah's community and Kentucky as a whole for "free slaves", compared to the rest of the states.

There were opportunities in other parts of Kentucky that Jeremiah could have taken advantage of. After the death of his mother, Jeremiah chose to stay in the community in which had grown up. He was familiar and comfortable with his surroundings. A self educated man, he used what he had learned from his mother's bible, to minister to the youth in his community. The youth having knowledge of written literature was puissant to Jeremiah. He became ordained at the age of 21. Pastor Isaiah allowed him to join the church board as assistant pastor. This position meant a lot to Jeremiah.

Times in Arkansas had proven to be hard for John Matthews, the brother of Bill Matthews, Jeremiah's boss. A year before the Great Depression began in 1929. John had been willed a 200 acre crop farm in Arkansas. Not knowing the first thing about farming, John asked his brother Bill if he could help him out. Bill requested that John come to Kentucky because he might have a solution. So, John set off to Kentucky to seek his brother's help.

It was a normal summer day for Jeremiah, when he was leaving the fields from working all day, when he was approached by a older non deterrent white man. The man removed his hat and extended his hand to greet Jeremiah. He then introduces himself to Jeremiah, "Hi you do? My name is John Matthews, please to meet you," says John.

"Much obliged. I don't mean no disrespect, but do you know me?" asks Jeremiah.

"Oh, son I'm sorry, your boss, Bill, is my brother," replies John.

"Okay, okay, please to meet you Mr. Matthews," says Jeremiah.

The two men began to walk. Jeremiah was thinking to himself that Mr. Matthews had never mentioned a brother before. And he quickly began to wonder what John wanted with him.

John leads the conversation, "Well Jeremiah, the reason I'm here in Kentucky is because a few months ago I wrote my brother Bill and asked him for some help. I recently took over my father-in-law's crop farm; close to 200 acres. And I tell you what, it's too much for me to handle. Working on the railroad for half my life, I know as much about farming as a blue bird knows about chopping wood. Bill let me know that he couldn't personally come, but he had a few hired hands that could possibly help me. The first name he said was yours. I know you've been in Kentucky all your life, but I would greatly appreciate if you would come to Arkansas to help me out," said John.

After John had finished speaking, Jeremiah stood there dumbfounded over the conversation. He took his hat off, scratched his head, and took a much needed sigh. "Well Mr. Matthews, I have earned a great deal of respect from your brother. He has always kept me working and always stood up for his workers if we had any trouble from the black and white nonsense that goes on in these here parts," says Jeremiah. He takes a brief pause and begins to continue speaking. "I don't believe he would ever steer me wrong, but this is a big step," says Jeremiah.

Even though Jeremiah was flattered by John's offer, he was a bit agnostic. He didn't know anything or anyone in Arkansas. Kentucky had been his only home. Although it wasn't perfect, he had grown to be accustomed to his environment. His mother and father were both buried there. The improbable thought of leaving heavily weighed on Jeremiah's mind.

"I know it's a lot to take in, but if I don't get somebody that knows what they're doing, I'll be up a creek without a paddle. I will pay you and the other three a descent wage and I do have a place for you boys to live," said John.

"You mentioned the other three. Who else is going?" asks Jeremiah.

"Well it's three boys that work with you, Harold, Ronnie, and Kent. I talked with them a little over a hour ago and they agreed to go, only if you would," replied John.

Jeremiah was eupeptic with the news that those three would consider going. Harold, Ronnie, Kent, and Jeremiah had been working together since they were very young. There were a plurality of things they had gone through together over the years. All four of the men had harvested strong bonds amongst themselves; therefore, for the first time, Jeremiah considered leaving Kentucky.

Extending his hand out to John, Jeremiah replied, "Well Mr. Matthews, I guess you might have yourself a deal. Just let me go and talk to the other boys first," said Jeremiah.

Shaking Jeremiah's hand, John responds, "Thank you! If you decided to go, we'll be leaving out the day after tomorrow."

"Good, that'll give me enough time to tie up some lose ends here," said Jeremiah.

The two men said their departing goodbyes and walked off in separate ways. Jeremiah had worked late that day; Harold, Ronnie, and Kent had gotten off earlier. With butterflies in his stomach, Jeremiah went to talk to the other three men.

Jeremiah's decision to go to Arkansas was heavily impacted by his friends' willingness to go. He anticipated the talk with the trio.

Out of the four young men, Harold was the only one that was married. He and his wife, Lillie, had two small children. They shared a house with Lillie's parents. Although they would miss their family, the thought of having their own house was tempting to them.

Ronnie, although not married, had been exclusively courting Lucille Carr, Pastor Isaiah's eldest daughter, for over two years. Moving to Arkansas would either make or break their relationship.

Kent, the same as with Jeremiah, was not married or in a relationship. Kent had courted his share of young ladies, without forming a monogamous relationship. His entire family was located in Kentucky; but he still looked forward to trying something different.

Once Jeremiah had arrived at Harold's, everyone was gathered outside. Nearly everyone in the town was there basking in the mutual excitement of the job offers for the four young men.

Jeremiah walks near and happily greets everyone. "Hello, everyone," says Jeremiah.

"Hello Jeremiah," responded the crowd. Everyone there was animatedly awaiting Jeremiah's answer.

"So Jay, did you talk to John Matthews?" asked Kent. Laughing and shaking Kent's hand, Jeremiah responds, "Yea, I did. Can you believe it?" he asked.

"I know man, we've been sitting here waiting until you came to see what you were going to do," said Kent.

Rubbing his forehead, Jeremiah responded, "Well boys, it's a big move for all of us, but I wouldn't mind a change. It won't hurt to at least try."

Jeremiah's response was exactly what the trio wanted to hear. They immediately began celebrating their decision to move to Arkansas. After the celebration, the four men went off to pack for their move. The day after tomorrow came expeditiously.

Jeremiah, with his belongings, closed the door to his somewhat commodious home in which he had shared with his mother and father for 25 years. Afterwards, he spoke with Pastor Isaiah and told him to do with the house as he pleased.

Jeremiah's house would later substitute as a school for the youth. In deciding to do this, Pastor Isaiah knew this would be what Jeremiah would have wanted.

Harold, Lillie, and their children, were packed and ready to leave when the time had come. Ronnie and Lucille were also packed. Pastor

Isaiah would only give the couple his blessing, if they did what was proper in his sight.

The night before they were to leave for Arkansas, Ronnie and Lucille, in a small ceremony, jubilantly and astutely wed. Although many blacks during this time and the time before this, where not married, Pastor Isaiah felt it necessary for Ronnie to marry Lucille before moving to Arkansas. Kent, as with the others, was packed and ready to go. He said his farewells to his family.

As they were leaving out, Bill approached Jeremiah. "Well son, I guess this is it. John will take care of you all, that's a promise. Now if you ever need to come back, I'll always have a spot for you. If you need anything later on down the road, you know how to get in touch with me," said Bill.

Jeremiah firmly grips Bill's hand. "Thank you, Mr. Bill. Thank you for never treating me like you were expected to treat me. Thank you sir," responded Jeremiah. Everyone there said their goodbyes and the group left Kentucky.

Chapter Four

His death took a toll on his family.

New Hope ...

Naomi was the third of five children, born to David and Bernice Rush. All five of the Wright children were born in a small town named New Hope. From the start of his marriage in 1903, to his unfortunate death in 1954, at the age of seventy, David was an assiduous provider for his family. He took a capacious delight in providing for his family. David inherited his work ethics from his father, Micah.

At the age of 17, David met Bernice. She was the daughter of a farmer and kitchen maid. Unlike David, Bernice did receive an education. Because of the culture of their town, she was only able to receive a minimal amount of education. This fact didn't hinder Bernice. Not only was she able to self educate, she also taught uneducated black children from her town and neighboring towns.

One cold day in 1903, David's mother, Jewel, asked him if he could go to the Wright's place to pick up his younger brother William. David didn't mind doing this because it meant a chance to get a glance at the Wright's oldest daughter, Bernice.

David, along with the other young unwed men from New Hope, was captivated over Bernice's beauty, as well as her disposition. Her skin was the color of warm caramel and as smooth as freshly made silk. Her hair was pitching black and fell to the arch in her back. Her big grey eyes were enrapturing. She had a smile that would warm the heart of the insusceptible. Just her speciousness tantalized all that came in contact with her. Although unacceptable, her beauty was appreciated by white men as well.

So on the day Jewel asked David to pick up his younger brother; he prepped himself before leaving the house. David was man of great stature. He was proportionally built. His facial structure was bold yet imperious. He stood six feet five inches tall. Every area of his bodily construction was rippled with muscles. As with Bernice, David was also admired by the opposite sex.

The entire walk from his house, to Bernice's house, David debated with himself on what he would say to Bernice. Every time he had previously saw her, she would be conversing with someone. He had never spoken to her. So his words had to be conspicuous in order for her to give him the time of day.

Once he arrived at the Wright's, David became visibly solicitous. He knew that he had to build enough courage simply to knock on the door. After he did, Jessie answered his knock. In an abstruse tone she asks, "What do you want boy!"

Although a petite woman, her demeanor immediately intimidated the six feet five inches tall, David. He quickly, but nervously responded, "How are you doing Mrs. Wright? My momma sent me to pick up William. Is he here?" asks David.

Jessie condescendingly responds, "What do you think boy. If she bought him over here this morning, then my guess would be that he's here. Just hold yourself right there and I'll fetch him. And don't you even think about stepping a foot into my house!" she yelled. She then slammed the door in David's face.

David took a sigh of relief. The entire town knew that Jessie was vitriolic, but seeing her in action, left David appalled. While David stood there waiting, Bernice's father, Don, walked up behind him and tapped him on the shoulder. Don startled David. Turning around to face Don, David says, "Ooh! Mr. Wright, you scared me."

"I'm sorry David; I didn't mean to scare you. How are you?" asked Don.

Shaking Don's hand, David replied, "I'm fine sir. Momma sent me to pick up William."

Don peaked over David's shoulder at the door to his house. "Son, let me talk to you before that woman comes back out. She's my wife; I've been with her since she was 15 years old. I have grown to love her, but that still doesn't mean that I have to love her ways. She's a little rough on the outside and she takes some getting used to," says Don.

Don continues to speak, "What I wanted to tell you is, I've noticed on several occasions how you looked at my Bernice. She's my youngest daughter and the joy of my life. I know she's not hard on the eyes. Lord knows, I've had my fair share of fools coming to me asking to court her. I haven't met a one yet, worth the silver on a nickel. But, I knew your daddy and I know your momma. I know that you are a hard worker, because I've seen you. Pay Jessie no never mind. Bernice is a smart girl and she's her own woman. If she takes a liking to you, then you both have my blessing," says Don.

Before David could respond, Don had vanished just as quickly as he had appeared.

The front door to the house swung open! It was William. Standing behind him was Bernice. She yelled in to Jessie, "Momma, I'm going to walk with David and William, I need to talk to Mrs. Jewel."

Like a bolt of lightning, Jessie was at the front door. "You need to be back here before dark. Look, boy, don't put your grubby hands on my daughter! You better have her back here before the sun goes down, you got that!" Jessie loudly says.

As big and strong as David was, at this very moment, he was petrified. "Yes mam, yes mam, I will," says David.

Jessie stood in the doorway shaking her head from side to side, staring at the three walk off out of her sight.

David took this opportunity to tell Bernice how he felt about her. Unbeknown to him, Bernice's feelings concerning him were mutual.

After this day, the two began to aggressively court one another. Three months later, the two were wed. After they married, the two moved next to Jessie and Don. David continued to farm and also picked up the skill of carpentry from Don. David worked very hard to make life as comfortable as he could for Bernice. She continued to teach children up until she gave birth to their first child.

In 1905, she gave birth to her first child, a boy, and they named him David, after his father. He was a blessing, not only to them, but to their parents as well.

Even though Jessie despised David, she loved her grandson. She was at Bernice and David's house more than they wanted. She was a great help to Bernice.

Three years after the birth of David Jr., a second son was born to Bernice and David, Samuel. He was loved just as much as his brother. Both brothers brought a since of contentment to both families.

Unfortunately, on Samuel's first birthday, his grandfather, Don, passed away. His death took a toll on his family. Although she didn't show it, Jessie was greatly heartbroken by Don's absence.

When Don died, his sons, Floyd and William, came home for his burial. Both brothers had moved away a few years earlier to work with Jessie's youngest brother. Unlike Floyd, William was excited about reuniting with his family.

The two men were not coming alone. Without Jessie's knowledge, William had married and had twin boys. He decided to bring his wife and children with him to introduce them to their family.

After Floyd and William arrived in New Hope, the first stop was their parents house. Seeing their mother was something they hadn't planned for. Jessie was there at the house when they arrived. Bernice and her family, along with neighbors, were there also to provide Jessie with unwanted comfort.

Floyd walked in first. He was welcomed by hugs and smiles from everyone in the house, except Jessie. He approached his mother, and gave her a kiss on the jaw and a nice warm hug.

"So, your daddy had to die in order for you to come home," says Jessie.

Floyd just stood there and looked at his mother grudgingly. He thought to himself that this was the very reason he had left New Hope, and didn't want to return. Jessie didn't have what someone would consider a motherly bond with any of her children.

"Floyd jokingly replied, "I love you to Jessie Wright!" He then joined in on the conversations of the others.

"Floyd, these are your nephews, David Jr. and Samuel," said Bernice. She handed her brother her two boys so he could hold them for the first time. Floyd started laughing and playing with his nephews.

"Where's William?" asked Bernice.

"He's coming in," replied Floyd.

Just then the door opened. William walked in holding his four year old twin boys, with his wife, Gertrude, directly behind him. As soon as he was noticed by everyone, they all instantly looked over to Jessie. In disbelief and utter shock, her mouth fell open.

"Hello everyone, including you Momma. This is Don Jr., this is William Jr., and this is my beautiful wife, Gertrude," said William, proudly.

They stood in the doorway waiting on a response from anyone; but there was only silence. Everybody just sat there in amazement. No one there knew that William had gotten married, let alone, had any children. After the initial shock, everyone except Jessie, warmly greeted William and his family with affectionate hellos and hugs. Bernice introduced her children to William and his family. The adults placed the children together, out of the way, so they could play together.

Jessie, with more hell in her than Satan himself, added her worthless two cents, "Wife! Children! You didn't have enough decency or respect to let me and your daddy know that you had a wife and kids!" proclaimed Jessie.

In a calm, stern, yet respectful tone, William responded, "Daddy did know I had a wife and kids. He was there when the twins were born. He was there when Gertrude and I named the twins, Don and William Jr. We didn't tell you about it because when I and Gertrude left New Hope, you told me if I married her that you wouldn't have anything to do with me. To cause you no unnecessary stress, we didn't tell you," says William.

His emotions were starting to get the best of him. He sternly continued to speak, "Now, I love you and I didn't come to bring you anymore heartache, but my wife and my boys, would be better off left out of your mouth! We came to say goodbye to My daddy. A daddy that never once judged me or turned his back on me or my family," said William.

Gertrude took a hold of William's arm to attempt to calm him down. The entire time they were married, she had never saw William this distraught.

After hearing what William had said to her, Jessie abruptly responded, "Everybody, I thank you for coming, but now I need to talk to my children, alone."

The neighbors all said goodbye. David gathered his children, along with Gertrude and her twins and went next door to his and Bernice's house. Neither David nor Gertrude wanted to disrespect Jessie; therefore, they willingly left.

Jessie then stood in the midst of her children. She did this when they were younger to intimidate them. This time it didn't work. Although the three sat there quietly, it wasn't out of fear anymore; it was out of respect for their mother.

Jessie began to speak, "I know that I have a reputation of being mean. I don't have a problem with that. But what I do have a problem with is when my own children don't want to have anything to do with me. When yall were growing up, I thought I was making the best decisions for you. Maybe I should have listened to Don more often. It used to make me mad as hell when he would tell me to 'take it easy on the kids.' My stubbornness wouldn't allow it," said Jessie.

Jessie sat down in a chair next to William and continued to speak, "I lost my best friend, the only person who put up with me. I wish that I could tell him that I'm sorry and take back all the hell I put him through. I know that I can't. I was sitting here, just now, with hatred in my heart for no reason, but Jesus! When I saw them beautiful, plumb twins, I felt built up pressure easing off my chest. I don't want you kids to not want to be around me. If you are willing, I want to be a part of all your families," said Jessie.

After she finished speaking, Jessie held her face and wept. Her three children were all emotionally overwhelmed by the loss of their father and by the gain of a new found relationship with their mother. This night was the ending of a sad chapter in each of their lives.

Don was peacefully laid to rest. Floyd went back north. William, Gertrude, and their twins, at Jessie's request, moved in with her. Jessie would prove to do as she said. Over the rest of the years of her life, Jessie formed strong bonds with her three children and their families.

Two years after the death of Don, Bernice gave birth to the first girl in the family, Naomi. She was a refreshing joy to the family. She also received extra attention, because she was the first girl to be born.

Over the next few years, the family grew larger. Bernice and David had two more children, Jonathan and Deborah. William and Gertrude also had more children, Norman and Leah. After Leah, there were no more children born of the children of Don and Jessie Wright.

At the young age of 13, Naomi was very active in church functions. It was a way she could read, sing, and travel; three things she loved to do. One Sunday, the pastor of her church announced that they would be traveling a couple counties south, for a fellow church program. The news of the trip mad Naomi intoxicatingly happy. Once she got the okay from Bernice and David, she was set to go.

A few days later, the group of church members safely arrived at their destination with no problem. Once there, Naomi was exhilarated to see so many girls her age. She was very outgoing; therefore, she didn't have a problem connecting with the other girls. There was instant agglutination between the groups of girls.

While laughing and communing with the other girls, Naomi looked up to see a young girl entering into the church. She hadn't noticed the girl before. There was something about the young girl that drew Naomi to her. So Naomi left from amongst the midst of the girls she was with to go introduce herself to the girl who had just entered into the church.

The girl was sitting alone on the back bench. "Hey, my name is Naomi. What's yours?" asks Naomi.

The girl bashfully responded, "Hi, my name is Alecta.

"Do you belong to this church?" asked Naomi.

"Yea, me, my momma, and my little brother," replied Alecta.

Feeling a little more at ease, Alecta continued talking, and said, "I knew another church was coming today. I was praying they would bring some girls my age."

"Your church has more girls than mine does," said Naomi.

"I know, but it's hard to talk to them. Most of the times they act like they don't even see me," says Alecta.

Naomi started to giggle."I don't mean to interrupt you, but I can't help from staring at you. Don't you think that me and you look just a like?" responded Naomi.

With a grin of agreement, Alecta said, "I was thinking the same thing, but I was scared to say something."

Over the period of time at the church, the two girls continued to get to know one another. They ended up spending the entire day together. As the church function was coming to an end, Alecta and Naomi didn't want their time together to end. Before leaving, they exchanged innocent hugs of amiability.

"I wish that you would come stay with me in the summer," said Alecta.

"I know! That would be so much fun. Since your mom is here, we can ask her first, and then if she says yes, I can ask my momma and daddy when I make it home," replies Naomi.

Alecta grabs Naomi by the hand and took off to find her mother. Through the crowd of people, Alecta spots her mother from behind. She tugged the back of her mother's skirt to get her attention. "Momma, this is my new friend Naomi," said Alecta.

Alecta's mother slowly turned around to respond to her. As she did, the first thing she saw was Naomi's face. Just as Alecta and Naomi, Alecta's mother was astonished by the girl's similarities. At first glance, Alecta's mother couldn't speak.

"Naomi, this is Mary Ann, my momma. Momma this Naomi my new friend from New Hope," says Alecta.

Reaching to shake Naomi's hand, Mary Ann says, "Hi Naomi, pleased to meet you. Mary Ann couldn't resist fixating on Naomi's physical appearance. She asked, "Naomi, are your parents with you?"

"No mam, my momma was busy and my daddy doesn't like going places with the church. He says they stay gone to long," replied Naomi.

Aborting their conversation, Alecta asked, "Momma, we wanted to know if Naomi could come stay with us for the summer?"

"Sure, that will be fine if it's okay with Naomi's mom and dad. By the way sweetie, what are your parent's names," asked Mary Ann.

"Bernice and David Rush," answered Naomi.

Just as Naomi responded, Alecta jokingly slapped her on the arm. "Naomi you are so silly. Your daddy's name is not David Rush. My daddy's name is David Rush," said Alecta. Her cheerful demeanor started to decline as she noticed her mother's expression.

Mary Ann stood there in the presence of Alecta and Naomi in a state of utter incredulity. She thought to herself that there had to be an explanation on why her husband and Naomi's father shared the same name. She stood there struggling with her explanations and reasoning on the situation. She thought, 'my David can't be her father.' She then began to get an abhorrent feeling in her stomach.

"Momma, do you know Naomi's daddy?" asked Alecta.

"I'm not sure baby," said Mary Ann.

The three stood there in brief confusion. Mary Ann proceeded to ask Naomi where exactly in New Hope she lived. Mary Ann also told

Naomi that herself, Alecta, and her son Micah, would come to visit with her and her family the following weekend. She let Naomi know not to say anything to her parents, because she wanted their visit to be a surprise.

Naomi and Alecta said goodbye to one another and the church group from New Hope left for home.

After Naomi's church group had left, one of the members of Mary Ann's church approached her. "Hello Sister Rush, how are you today?" asked Sandra.

Precipitously, Mary Ann responded, "I'm fine; I was just on my way home. Alecta go get your brother so we can go," said Mary Ann.

She started to walk off when Sandra grabbed her by the arm, almost inaudibly Sandra said, "Yea Sister Rush, I don't me any harm, but me and Sister Daniels was wondering who that child was that Alicia was with." With an offensively curious grin, Sandra went on to say, "Hmm, she sure looks like your husband."

Sandra's comments upset Mary Ann a great deal. She felt as if she was already a target for gossipers because she and David were not "legally married". In a tempestuous tone, Mary Ann said, "Well Sandra, you don't look like the first lady, but if I'm not mistaken, I did hear Pastor Jones call her by your name!"

Sandra turned her nose up and rolls her eyes at Mary Ann and then walked off. Mary Ann animatedly waited for her husband, David to return home, she had some questions of her own for him.

Chapter Five

He got more than a job when he was in Longpoint.

Naomi's Exciting News ...

ONCE NAOMI ARRIVED HOME from her trip with the church, she went on a search to find her mother, only to find out that she wasn't home. Jessie was there attending to Jonathan and Deborah. Naomi ran over to Jessie, nearly knocking her down.

"Granny, where's momma?" asked Naomi.

Trying to calm Naomi down, Jessie responded, "Naomi, settle down before you wake up Jonathan and Deborah. She's not here. She'll be back a little later. She had something to take care of. What is it? Why are you so happy?" asked Jessie.

"Granny, I'm not supposed to say anything, but I can't help it!" replied Naomi.

Jessie sat down in a chair and gently pulled Naomi onto her lap. "Now, what is it that you're not supposed to say?" asked Jessie.

Naomi began to tell Jessie about her trip. "Well Granny, I met a girl named Alecta. We look just alike, like D.J. and William Jr. I met her momma. Guess what else Granny?" asked Naomi.

"What else baby," asked Jessie.

Naomi mirthfully responds, "David Rush is Alecta's daddy's name to!" said Naomi.

Jessie meekly pushed Naomi onto her feet and held her by both arms. Shaking Naomi, Jessie responded, "Okay baby. Now calmly tell me what you just said again."

Naomi calmly responded, "David Rush is Alecta's daddy's name, just like mine. Alecta, her momma, and her little brother are coming to visit next weekend. Her momma told me not to say anything to anyone about them coming, because she wants it to be a surprise.

Jessie then stood up! She began to pace the floor, up and down. She angrily started swinging her arms back and forth.

"Granny, are you okay?" asked Naomi.

"Yea baby, Granny is fine. Now, tell Granny what else you know about Alecta and her family. Wait a minute! Where was her daddy?" asked Jessie.

"Oh, he wasn't there. He works on the railroad. Alecta said he be gone all the time," replied Naomi.

"How old is Alecta?" asked Jessie.

"Alecta is 12 and her brother Micah is 11. Why, Granny?" asks Naomi.

Hearing this news from Naomi infuriated Jessie. She didn't let her rage show physically to her granddaughter. "Where do they live?" asked Jessie.

"In Longpoint, why, do you know them Granny?" asked Naomi.

"No baby, I was just asking. What's Alecta's mother's name?" asked Jessie.

"Mary Ann Rush. Granny, do you think they are kin to daddy?" asked Naomi.

"I doubt it. A lot of people have the same last name. Do Granny a favor; take this pot of peas over to your Aunt Gertrude's for me. She's been waiting on them. Before you go, let me tell you something. We're not going to tell your momma about Alecta and her momma coming. You know how your momma is about surprises. I'll help you get everything ready before they come, okay baby," said Jessie.

Walking towards the front door with the pot of peas, Naomi responded, "okay Granny. Can you cook a chocolate cake for next weekend, it's Alecta's favorite."

"Sure baby, whatever you want," replied Jessie.

After Naomi left, Jessie's frustrations began to show. Crying, she slammed both her fists onto the table! She sat down at the table, pounding her fists and rocking back and forth in the chair.

In a rage, she began to talking aloud, "Don! Didn't I tell you that this black beast was no good for Bernice! You know that David Rush and Bernice's David Rush are one in the same. When you died, he told us that he had got a carpentry job in Longpoint. Yea, right! He got more than a job when he was in Longpoint. The boy's name is Micah. Only a fool wouldn't know that he named that boy after his daddy Micah. This tired, lying, no good son of a bitch! Don, as you and God is my only witnesses, Mrs. Mary Ann and Mr. Rush will answer to me for this shit! My baby can't find about this," exclaimed Jessie.

Once Naomi returned from her aunt's house, she stood outside the door of her house. She could hear Jessie banging against something. Instead of opening the door, she pressed her ear against it. She heard her grandmother say that Mary Ann and Mr. Rush would answer to her for this. Naomi didn't understand what her grandmother meant, but she did know never to question Jessie about anything.

Meanwhile, Back in Longpoint ...

The following Wednesday after the church from New Hope had visited Longpoint, Alecta was still excited about meeting Naomi. Once Alicia saw her mother walking up the road, she ran to meet her. "Hey momma how was your day?" she asked.

"Oh, it was fine Alecta, just long. Did you and your brother give Richard a hard time while I was at work?" asked Mary Ann.

"No momma. He let us help him peel apples!" said Alecta.

"Okay good girl. Let's stop and get your brother." said Mary Ann.

Mary Ann and Alecta stopped by her neighbor Richard's house to pick up Micah. "Hey Richard, where they any trouble?" asked Mary Ann.

"No, they don't bother me. They both should be full of apples though," jokingly said Richard.

"Thanks again Richard. Come on kids let's go home so you can get dressed for bed," said Mary Ann.

Once Mary Ann, Alecta, and Micah dressed down for bed, they gathered in the front room to spend some quality time together before going to sleep. Micah lay on the floor and began playing with his toy trucks his dad had previously bought for him, while Alecta snuggled next to Mary Ann on the couch.

"Momma wasn't Naomi really nice?" asked Alecta.

Mary Ann tightly snuggled with Alecta, looked down at her and kissed her on the forehead. "Yes, she was. We are going to visit her the weekend, but don't get your hopes up, okay," said Mary Ann.

"Okay momma I won't," replied Alecta.

"Alecta, how old is Naomi?" asked Mary Ann.

"She is 13, her oldest brother D.J. is about to be 20, then there's Sam, he's almost 16, then there's Jon, he's nine, and her little sister Deb is seven. She has a big family, don't she momma?" asked Alecta.

"Wow! She does have a big family," said Mary Ann.

After listening to Alecta name off all of Naomi's siblings, Mary Ann became bothered. Her instincts made her suspicious about all David had told her over the years concerning the true status of his relationship with his wife.

When Mary Ann met David in 1909, he told her that he was married and had to small boys, a three year old and a one year old. He never told Mary Ann his wife's name. To Mary Ann's satisfaction, David assured her that he and his wife were not in love with each other anymore and they wouldn't have any more children because of this. After Mary Ann had Alecta, she became content with her and David's relationship.

Now after actually seeing Naomi and learning of David having children with his wife, after he met her, made Mary Ann very upset.

Mary Ann didn't know if David was coming home or not this particular day. She had grown accustomed to him not showing up for weeks at a time. But whenever he came home this time, she was ready to get to the bottom of this.

Alecta eventually fell asleep in Mary Ann's arm. Micah had fallen asleep on the floor. Mary Ann carefully led Alecta to her bed. Once she had tucked Alecta in, she went back and carried Micah into where Alecta was asleep. Then she stood in the doorway and looked down at her children lay peacefully sleeping, and whispered, "Goodnight my little angels."

For the first time in her and David's relationship, Mary Ann felt as though her soul was being convicted. Her guilt became too overpowering for her conscious. All of a sudden, she fell to her knees! She then began to speak aloud, "Jesus, please forgive me for my sins. I knew that David was married, but I still chose to lay with him and conceive his children. Jesus, do to me as you please, but I beg you not to let my children find out what I have done," said Mary Ann.

Her prayer was interrupted by a loud knock on the door. She wiped the tears from her face to answer the door. "Who is it," she asked.

"Mary Ann, this is Roberta Rush. I'm David's cousin," said the woman at the door.

Mary Ann thought to herself for a brief second, 'David never mentioned a cousin Roberta.' She skeptically opens the door. Once the door was open, Mary Ann didn't know if this lady was related to David or not. She didn't recognize the man standing behind the lady either.

"You are Mary Ann, right? The one that supposed to be married to David Rush," asked the woman.

"Yes I am the one, married, to David Rush. Come in and have a seat. David never mentioned you before," said Mary Ann.

The situation unexpectedly shifted downhill. In a muscular tone of speech, the man said to Mary Ann, "No, I need you to have a seat!"

Now feeling perturbed over the strangers in her house, Mary Ann said, "Excuse me. Who are you people? Why are you here?" asked Mary Ann.

The man pushed his companion to the side and very forcefully pushed Mary Ann onto the couch! He then proceeds to pull out a large knife from his coat and stoutly says, "Shut your damn mouth! I told you to sit your ass down," yelled the man.

In a panic, Mary Ann pleaded, "Please don't hurt me. I don't have any money."

The man then pulls his hand back behind his head and brings it down with abundant force against Mary Ann's face! The impact from the man's hand knocked her to the floor. She then palms her face as if to protect it from being struck again.

Arrogantly standing over Mary Ann, the man loudly said, "The only thing that you have that I want, is your blood and the blood of those bastard kids you got by David," said the man.

Mary Ann attempted to rise to her feet only to be pushed back down to the floor by the man's foot. He pressed his foot heavily on her back.

Sobbing and pleading for her and her children's lives, Mary Ann said, "Please don't hurt my children. They haven't hurt anybody. Please don't! Why are you doing this to us?"

The man then bends down to Mary Ann's' level and powerfully snatched her head back! With his mouth pressed against her ear, he said to Mary Ann, "Look, you rotten hoe, you can't just go around playing house with a man who doesn't belong to you. Was you begging for your life when you was sleeping with Bernice's husband? Yeah! That's right hoe, Bernice's husband, not your damn husband!" said the man.

Still at the same level as Mary Ann, the man spit directly on her face and vehemently slammed her head into the floor! Mary Ann's head hit the floor so hard that the front of her skull was exposed.

In a delusional frame of mind, Mary Ann, while whimpering, began pleading with Jesus to save her and her children.

The man was now standing over Mary Ann. He heard her pleas, and says, "Boo Hoo, hoe. Was you crying and calling on Jesus when you opened your legs to a married man? Huh?" exclaimed the man.

The man's woman companion says to him, "Look, we need to do this shit so we can go! You told me that I was getting a drank, and you still aint gave me nothing to drank. I'm thirsty and I been in these boondocks all damn day. Come on now, my nerves getting bad!" said the woman.

"Alright, alright, calm your drunk ass down! Get over here and hold this hoe down," the man stated.

The woman walks over to where the man was standing and where Mary Ann was laying on the floor. After he moved his foot from Mary Ann's back, the woman put her foot onto to Mary Ann.

"Here, take the knife. Don't let her up! If she moves, cut her damn throat," said the man.

Mary Ann was strong enough to hold her head up and see the man heading toward the room where her children were asleep. "Where are you going," shouted Mary Ann.

The woman used her foot to push Mary Ann's face back onto the floor. "Shut up, shut up, shut up! Shit, you making me nervous," said the woman.

As the man continued towards where Mary Ann's children were, he turned his head and looked back at Mary Ann and smiled. He then pulls a pistol from inside his coat and holds it up for Mary Ann to see it. He then starts laughing, and says to her, "Now you pay attention to this! I'm what happen to folks when they decide to have kids with somebody else's husband." He slowly enters the room where the kids were sleeping.

Mary Ann listened and saw him raise his pistol and enter the room where her kids were. Crawling on her stomach, with the woman's foot still on her back, Mary Ann pleaded for her children, "No! Please don't hurt them! Please, please," she said while crying.

The woman tried as hard as she could to hold Mary Ann down with her foot, but to no prevail. Mary Ann stood to her feet! Limping with her arms stretched out towards her children, Mary Ann hears a shot! "No!" she screamed.

Mary Ann then fell to the floor. Her head injury had caused her to lose strength from her body. Attempting to reach her children, her efforts didn't pay off. The woman walks up to Mary Ann while she was crawling on the floor. The woman then sat on Mary Ann's back and pulls her hand back over her head, with the knife intact. She then brings the knife down, stabbing Mary Ann in the back of her neck seven times.

Just as the knife went into Mary Ann's neck for the eighth time, the man fired a second shot.

The man, with the gun in his hand, pulled the tip of the gun to his mouth and blew it. In a evil tone, he said, "Sorry kids, it had to be done."

He then left the room and walked over to the woman sitting on Mary Ann's back. The woman was covered in Mary Ann's blood. The man put his pistol back inside his coat and says, "I hope you didn't kill her before I shot them kids."

"No I didn't. She heard you shoot both of them. Are you happy now?" she asked.

The man reached down and helped the woman to her feet. Excited over what they had done, he kissed the woman directly on her lips and said, "Damn right I'm happy! Don't mess with my folks. Umm, that hoe's blood tastes better than that old boy out of Chicago. Now, let's go get your drank!"

Chapter Six

*Naomi soon realized that her grandmother was
the pure quintessence of wickedness.*

Is Alecta Really Coming …?

OVER THE NEXT FEW days after returning from her church trip to
Longpoint, Naomi readied herself for the arrival of Alecta. Naomi had
done as her grandmother had told her and not said anything to her
mother or father about Alecta. As it got closer to the weekend, Naomi
began to wonder if Alecta was coming.

Finally the weekend had come, but to no avail, she hadn't come.
Days turned to weeks, weeks turned into months, still no Alecta. Naomi
was angry at Alecta and Mary Ann for not coming as they said they
would. Jessie never mentioned her to Naomi and she never brought up
her name to Jessie. In the back of her mind, Naomi always wondered if
she would ever see Alecta again.

As the years went on, Naomi gradually forgot about Alecta and her
mother. She had never mentioned Alecta to her parents or brought her
name back up to her grandmother. Naomi always wondered in the back
of her mind if she and Alecta were related in some kind of way.

At the age of 17, Naomi began teaching, as her mother had done
before her. She took great pride in teaching. She taught the local children
in the towns only black church.

On a Friday evening, Naomi was straightening up behind her

students, when a fellow church member walked in. "Hello Naomi," said Debbie.

Naomi stopped what she was doing and responded, "Hello Mrs. Debbie. I'm just straightening up some before I go home. How are you?"

"I'm fine. I came to do the same thing. We have a visiting church coming this Sunday," said Debbie.

"Oh, that sounds exciting. Where is the church visiting from?" asked Naomi.

"Longpoint." said Debbie.

"Okay. We went there four years ago and I really enjoyed the program," said Naomi.

"Oh my, I did to," said Debbie.

"Well, I'm going to hang around a little longer to help you get things ready for Sunday, if you don't mind," said Naomi.

"No! It's really sweet of you to offer to help me. Lord knows I need all the help I can get," said Debbie.

The two women continued to clean the church in great depth. While Naomi was busy cleaning, she thought back about the time she had met Alecta Rush. She hoped that Alecta or her mother, Mary Ann, would be coming with the church group on Sunday.

Sunday came quickly for Naomi. Once the church had arrived, she looked around for Alecta and her mother. Unfortunately she didn't see either of them. After the program ended, Naomi approached a young girl from the visiting church. "Hi! Linda, is it? Do you remember me?" asked Naomi.

Gazing at Naomi for a brief second, Linda gaily responded, "Naomi! Of course I remember you. We had fun when you were at our church."

The two young women commence to catching up on things that have happened since they last saw each other. They carried their conversation outside. "So Linda, I was wondering why I didn't see Alecta or her momma. Do they go to church somewhere else?" asked Naomi.

Linda's immediate reaction baffled Naomi. With a enormous quantity of sadness in her voice, Linda said, "Oh my goodness, you don't know what happened to them?"

Naomi became uneasy after Linda spoke. "Linda, what do you mean, what happened?" asked Naomi.

"Come here. Let's sit down on this bench," said Linda. The two of them sat down and Linda leads the conversation. "Well, the Sunday that your church came to visit, was the last time anybody from the church saw them alive," said Linda.

Sobbing uncontrollably, Naomi says, "No! I mean, what happened?" asked Naomi.

Reliving the tragedy, Linda went on to say, "The day after you left, Mrs. Mattie, a lady that cleaned houses with Mary Ann, stopped by as usual to get her so they could walk to work together. She stood outside knocking for about 30 minutes or so. Nobody answered the door so she went next door to see if they had seen her. Richard, Mary Ann's neighbor, told Mrs. Mattie that he hadn't seen her all morning. He said the night before, he saw a woman and a man going into Mary Ann's house. The reason he paid attention to them was the fact that he had never seen them before. Then him and Mrs. Mattie walked back over to Mary Ann's," said Linda.

Linda continued to tell Naomi what Richard and Mattie had witnessed. "Mrs. Mattie said Richard didn't knock, he just walked in. When they both got inside, they saw Mary Ann lying on the floor. Richard walked over to see if she was breathing, but she wasn't. She was dead!" said Linda.

Naomi sat there listening to Linda in complete disbelief. "Linda, are you serious?" asked Naomi.

Linda placed her hand on Naomi's knee to comfort her. "Naomi, I'm sorry, but that's not the worst of it," said Linda.

"Oh my goodness, what else?" asked Naomi.

Linda continued her story, "Mattie stayed with Mary Ann's body while Richard went to check the rest of the house. When he made it to the back of the house, he saw Alecta and Micah lying beside each other dead," said Linda.

"Linda, I can't believe this!" shouted Naomi.

"I know. It was a shock to everybody. It was bad enough to kill Mary Ann, but to kill two kids was just too much," said Linda.

"Okay, wait! What about their dad, was he there?" asked Naomi.

"No, he was out of town as usual. Nobody knew how to get in touch with him. He come showing up two days later. The police questioned him. After they did, they said he couldn't have done it. His boss told them that he was at work when this happened," said Linda.

Naomi was baffled over this news. "Okay, so what about the man and the woman that Richard saw," said Naomi.

"Richard told the police that the man he saw was about six feet, not really old, but not young either and the woman was about five feet, small build and looked the same age as the man. He said that he had never seen the man or the woman in town before," said Linda.

"How was they killed?" asked Naomi.

"Mary Ann was stabbed in the neck a lot of times. Alecta and Micah were both shot in the head," said Linda.

Naomi dropped her head into the palms of her hands and began crying. She felt so guilty for being angry at Alecta and Mary Ann. She raised her head and turned to Linda with a meek grin. "You know, they were supposed to have come and visited me and my family the following weekend after we left. I feel so bad now, because I got mad at them for not showing up," said Naomi.

Linda reached out to comfort Naomi. With reassurance, Linda said, "Don't beat yourself up Naomi. You didn't know. You want to know what else. Even though the police said he didn't kill them, they did find out that he was married to someone else. Mary Ann wasn't even his real wife," said Linda.

"Say what!" shouted Naomi.

"Yeah, he has another wife and kids. The police said that he was going back and forth from his wife to Mary Ann for many years. After they were all killed, he never came back. And the police arrested a man from another town that they said Mary Ann was going with. Richard told the police that the man and woman that he saw were the only people who went inside that house that night," said Linda.

Naomi became ill to the stomach. Linda's story was getting even odder. She then dreadfully asked Linda, "What was David's real wife's name?"

"If I remember correctly, I think it was Bernice. Yeah, that's it, Bernice Rush, that's her name," said Linda.

All of a sudden, Naomi jumped up from where she sat and dashed off into the woods behind the church.

Linda sat there in a state of confusion. She soon realized that Naomi wasn't coming back. She then returned to her church group and they left New Hope to return to Longpoint.

Naomi didn't have a clue to where she was running. She ran until her legs became tired. Eventually she ended up in the middle of the woods behind the church. After she was physically exhausted, she fell flat out on her back.

Crying and disgusted over what Linda had just told her, she began to speak aloud, "Jesus, are you there," she shouts in desperation. "Oh my God, Daddy has to be the same David Rush. How is it that I and Alecta looked just a like? How is that her daddy's other wife has the same name as my momma?" said Naomi.

She then implores to God and says, "No, No! Please don't let it be. Daddy please do not be Alecta's daddy," she begged.

After laying on the ground for over an hour, Naomi became capable enough to physically walk home. Upon her arrival Naomi was very upset. Her father wasn't at home, but her mother was. Naomi stood off out of sight, intensely admiring her mother. She thought to herself, 'this can't be true. Look how happy she looks. She would never do anything to hurt daddy. How could he do this to her, how could he do this to us.'

Naomi wanted so bad to talk to her mother about this, but she couldn't bring herself to disrespecting her mother. Things in her family of this sort, was for adults only.

Jessie wondered upon Naomi standing admiring Bernice. She walked up close to Naomi and whispered, "Baby, what are you doing?"

"Granny, you scared me! I was just looking at Momma braid Deb's hair," said Naomi.

"Did you have a good time at church?" asked Jessie.

"Yes mam. Could we go outside? I really need to talk to you," said Naomi.

Jessie takes a hold of Naomi's hand and the two of them walked outside and sat on the swing underneath the large oak tree. Jessie looked over at Naomi and said, "What's wrong? I can tell that you've been crying."

Naomi takes a brief pause to prevent her tears from falling. Once she had composed herself, she then said, "Granny the worst thing in the world just happened."

Jessie put one arm around Naomi and placed her free hand on Naomi's knee. "Okay, you're scaring me," said Jessie.

"A girl from a visiting church just told me that my friend Alecta, her momma, and her brother were all killed," said Naomi.

"What!" shouted Jessie?

"Yes mam. Do you remember a few years ago when I told you about meeting a girl that looked just like me named Alecta? Remember, I told you that our daddies had the same name," said Naomi.

Jessie's face went impassive. "Yes, I remember. This girl you're talking about, is the same girl you met? Are you sure that it's not a different girl?" asked Jessie.

"Yes Granny. She also told me that Alecta's daddy had another wife and her name is Bernice Rush!" said Naomi.

Jessie abruptly released her hold on Naomi and looked off. "It's not my Bernice!" said Jessie.

Naomi pulled Jessie's face around to look at her. "Granny it is momma. Daddy has been working out of town since Papa died. I didn't pay attention back then, but daddy said he was working in Longpoint. That's were Alicia and her family lived. I'm not stupid!" "He didn't kill them, but momma will die if she found out," said Naomi.

Jessie tensely responded, "How do you know for sure? Don't just instantly think that your daddy is the same man that was married to that dead woman."

Naomi did not believe what Jessie was saying. She certainly knew that she and Alecta had the same father. There were just too many coincidences.

"Okay, what if he is the same David, how do you know that he didn't kill them?" asked Jessie.

"A man Mary Ann was supposedly going with was arrested," said Naomi.

"It doesn't matter who stabbed her," said Jessie, before she stopped herself from talking.

"Wait a minute Granny, how do you know she was stabbed?" asked Naomi.

Jessie stood and took a few steps, with her back to Naomi. Looking dumbfounded, she said, "Uh, you told me."

"No I didn't Granny! I didn't tell you how any of them got killed. Granny please, I asked you a question!" said Naomi.

"Look at here, little black girl, you better take your tone down! If you didn't tell me then I must have heard it somewhere, that's all," said Jessie.

For some reason, Naomi didn't believe Jessie. She thought back to the night she had stood outside the door listening to Jessie shout out, 'Mary Ann and Mr. Rush would answer to her for this.' She didn't know what it meant then, but she now assumed that it had something to do with this situation. She couldn't bring herself to believe that Jessie had anything to do with killing somebody. "Granny, please tell me that you didn't know that daddy was messing with Mary Ann," begged Naomi.

Jessie looked directly at Naomi and said, "David is a man, not Jesus. A man will do anything. I don't put anything passed him. Now, when he married my daughter, I told him then, that he better not hurt her. I told him the day that they got married that if he did he would live to regret it. David or nobody else is going to hurt my child. Yes, I do believe that he was with that home wrecker and then had the nerve to have those two bastard children. When you do something wrong to somebody it comes back on you, double fold," said Jessie.

Jessie walked a little further, and continued to speak to Naomi. "I can honestly say that I never met that woman or her children, but I'm not going to stand here and pretend like I give a damn that they are dead. They arrested somebody, therefore the situation is closed! Now, as for you, I told your daddy not to hurt my child, and I'm telling you the same thing. Don't open your mouth to your momma about that woman and her children. Do you understand what Granny is saying," asked Jessie.

Naomi's sorrow quickly turned to fear. She had always heard the horror stories about Jessie before she had children, but she had never actually saw Jessie's evil side. Naomi did know, whenever Jessie said something, she meant it.

Trembling, Naomi responded, "Okay Granny, I won't say anything. I couldn't stand seeing Momma get hurt."

Jessie reached over and coldly hugged Naomi. "Good girl," said Jessie.

After talking to Jessie, Naomi soon realized that her grandmother was the pure quintessence of wickedness. After this conversation with Jessie, Naomi didn't now know if she did have anything to do with the three murders or not.

Jessie wasn't the only person Naomi avoided; she started avoiding her father, David also. Naomi couldn't understand her feelings, but she couldn't accept her father being unfaithful to her mother.

After finding out of Alecta's murder and the conversation she had with Jessie, about Alecta's murder, Naomi chose to occupy much of her time at the church. Being at the church comforted her. The most time she spent at home was when David was out of town and when Jessie wasn't visiting.

Chapter Seven

He captured her face and pulled it to his! His lips and hers touched! Then they began to passionately kiss!

Jeremiah and Naomi Meet ...

IT WAS A NORMAL Sunday morning in the life of 17 year old Naomi Rush. After eating breakfast with her family, they all left for church. Once there, as usual, Naomi led the Sunday lesson for the smaller children in the church. When the Sunday lessons where over, Naomi and the children joined the rest of the congregation for the sermon.

As Nomi walked to her seat, Leah came up beside her and grabbed a hold of her arm. Leah was Naomi's Uncle William and Aunt Gertrude's only daughter; Naomi's best friend. The two girls walked to their seats together. Leah began to giggle quietly, and said, "Did you see the new members? I heard they're from Kentucky. They're working for Old Man Matthews. Look! Those two there don't have a woman with them. One for you and one for me," said Leah.

Naomi bashfully looked up at the two men that Leah spoke of. She puts her hand over her mouth and smiled. "Leah, hush! You're terrible," replied Naomi.

"Well what do you think?" asked Leah.

"I think we should talk about it after Pastor Mitchell gives his sermon," replied Naomi.

As everyone in the church attentively focused on the pastor giving his sermon, Naomi's eyes wondered onto one of the men. She said to herself, 'Forgive me Father, he is the most handsome man I've ever laid my eyes on.' The man was a refreshing sight to Naomi. As with her mother, Naomi was also very beautiful. She was admired by all of the young men in her town.

As Naomi sat there fixated on the strange man, he turned around and noticed her looking at him. He looked directly into her eyes and smiled. She returned the smile and shamefully held her head down. She couldn't explain the instant attraction she had for him, but she liked it.

Once services had ended, Naomi and Leah walked outside to converse with fellow church members. "Naomi, Naomi! Could you come here for a second," asked Pastor Mitchell.

Naomi heard the pastor. She grabbed Leah by the arm and the two went to see what he wanted. Before she made it to where the pastor was standing, she noticed the man and some more strangers standing with the pastor. In a state of nervousness, she squeezed Leah's arm.

"Naomi, Leah, I want to introduce you to our new members," said Pastor Mitchell.

The two young women stood there before Pastor Mitchell and the new members. Both of the young women were nervous, but were eager to meet the two men who didn't have women with them.

"Naomi, Leah, this is Brother Harold and Sister Lillie Roberts. These little ones here are their children, Leona and George," said Pastor Mitchell. Both girls warmly greeted the Roberts family.

"Okay, this is Brother Ronnie and Sister Lucille Jones," said Pastor Mitchell. As with the Roberts, the girls warmly greeted the Jones'. Naomi knew that it was time to meet the stranger she had shared a smile with earlier.

"This is Pastor Jeremiah Strong and Brother Kent Black. Pastor Strong was assistant pastor at his church home in Kentucky. I told him that we will be more than happy to add him to our church board when and if he wants too," said Pastor Mitchell.

Jeremiah stepped directly up to Naomi, removed his hat, and took her hand, and said, "Very, nice to meet you Naomi."

Naomi holding tightly onto Jeremiah's hand, clears her throat, and said, "Very, nice to meet you Pastor Strong."

"No, please call me Jeremiah," he said.

"Okay, very nice to meet you Jeremiah," said Naomi.

At first glance, at first touch, there was a mutual connection between Jeremiah and Naomi. The second Jeremiah saw her in the church; he knew that she would be his wife one day. He made a vow to himself inside the church that he wouldn't give up until she was his wife. What he didn't know was that Naomi made the very same vow to herself upon seeing him.

"Naomi, Pastor Strong was very active in his church in Kentucky," said Pastor Mitchell.

Jeremiah, still holding onto Naomi's hand, said, "I would love to talk with you more about the different things I did for my church."

Naomi cheerfully responded, "Jeremiah I would love that. Since you and your company are new here, my family and I would love to have you for Sunday dinner."

Jeremiah looked over at his company and they all agreed to go to Naomi's house for dinner.

"We would love to," said Jeremiah.

Just as Naomi was about to give him directions to her house, Pastor Mitchell stepped up. "Oh yes Naomi. We, would love to come for dinner," said Pastor Mitchell.

"Why of course Pastor. If you don't mind showing them the way to the house, say around five or so," said Naomi.

Grabbing Naomi's hand from Jeremiah and shaking it, Pastor Mitchell replied, "I sure will, I sure will. We will see you at five or so. Oh by the way, do you think Sister Rush made her famous fried chicken?"

"Yes sir, I quit sure she did," said Naomi.

Jeremiah was overly excited about having dinner with Naomi and her family. He wanted to take this time with Naomi, getting to know her.

Once Jeremiah, his company, and Pastor Mitchell arrived at Naomi's, Pastor Mitchell lead the blessing of the food and everyone began eating. While everyone was eating, Jeremiah and Naomi, sitting next to each other, took the opportunity to get to know one another; so did Leah and Kent.

Since Ronnie and Harold where both married, they joined the other married couples, William, Gertrude, David, and Bernice. Kent,

Leah, Jeremiah, and Naomi went off by themselves as well, to get better acquainted.

From that Sunday afternoon and on, Jeremiah and Naomi became inseparable. In November of that year, Jeremiah and Naomi where wed.

Jeremiah was at his home, which he shared with Kent, getting dressed to go to his wedding ceremony, when John Matthews knocked on the door.

"Hey son, how's it going? I'm not going to keep you. I need to give you a couple of things and I'll be on my way," said John.

Jeremiah invited John inside. They sat down next to each other. John passed an envelope over to Jeremiah and said, "Bill sent this to you. I had written him a little while ago to let him know that everything was well with you and the others. I told him you were getting married to a girl from here. So he wrote back and asked me to give you this."

Jeremiah opened the envelope and inside was one hundred dollars. Jeremiah was speechless! After a brief delay in their conversation, he asked, "Mr. Matthews, what is this?"

"Well son, Bill told me that he owed you more than that. He said that this money was a gift for being so good to him," said John.

"Mr. Matthews, this is just about the nicest thing anybody has done for me," replied Jeremiah.

"Why boy, you deserve it. I had my doubts at first, you being colored and all. But now I see what my brother was talking about. Color doesn't mean anything when you find a good friend. I haven't had to ask you to do anything, you just do it. Even with times being so damn hard, you saved my farm," said John.

Jeremiah sat there in pure disbelief. He couldn't understand why he had been so blessed to work for, not one but two white men that didn't abuse him or mistreat him. Jeremiah saw many black people around him in Kentucky and Arkansas heavily impacted by the disease called Racism. Both John and Bill where criticized by their white peers because they helped blacks instead of punishing them for the color of their skin.

"Mr. Matthews, I am much obliged to you and Mr. Bill. If I hadn't met him, I would have never met you. And if I had never met you, I wouldn't have met Naomi. I look forward to breathing, just so I can see her face. So I feel like I owe you and Mr. Bill," said Jeremiah.

Bill started to laugh and said, "Good, I guess we need each other then. One more thing before I go. I own that section up the road where those colored folks live. Now one of my houses up there is empty. It's small, but I've seen your carpentry skills. You can add on to it little by little until you get it how you want it to be. I would like for you to have that house as your own. It's yours, don't give me a dime. I know you about tired of shacking up with Kent."

Jeremiah was flabbergasted over both men's generosity. He gratefully accepted both gifts.

After they were married, Jeremiah and Naomi moved into the house given to them by John. He took the money that Bill had given him, along with the 77 dollars he had been saving, and gradually improved the house.

The night that Jeremiah and Naomi were wed, was a special moment for the both of them. Both were virgins and both had dreamed of this very moment.

Both of them were nervous. Naomi left from Jeremiah's presence to change her clothes. Once in a different room, she removed the dress that she was wearing. She then took a small jar of scented cream from her bag. She placed a small amount of cream into her hands and rubbed them together. Starting at her face, Naomi slowly rubbed the cream onto her body. From her face, she went down to her neck. From her neck she proceeded down the rest of her body, careful not to miss a inch of skin. She desperately wanted her husband to be pleased with the softness and the smell of her bare body.

Once Naomi had applied enough cream to her satisfaction, she removed her dressing gown from her bag. Her mother had made the gown especially for Naomi's wedding night. The gown was made of a soft white material and the edges were trimmed with lace. Naomi slid the gown over her head and the bottom of the gown touched the floor. The gown fit perfectly to every sculptured curve of her body. She then removed the two pins from her hair that had been holding her hair up in a bun. Her hair was black as the darkest night, soft as freshly picked cotton, and had a quaint smell of a field of flowers. She was absolutely ravishing.

Jeremiah stood in the next room patiently awaiting on Naomi to come in and get him. There were many thoughts going through his mind as he stood there.

Naomi walked back to where Jeremiah stood. Jeremiah legs weakened, his heart raced, and his many thoughts vanished. The forgotten thoughts were replaced by the essence of his wife's beauty. He extended his hand out to her. She graciously walked over to him, where her hands rested in his.

Jeremiah intensely gazed into Naomi's eyes. With tears of joy, now flowing from his face, he said, "You, are completely beautiful. I've waited on you my entire life. Seeing you at this moment makes me realize that my wait was not in vain."

Naomi took her hand and tenderly wiped the tears from Jeremiah's face. As her hand rested upon his face, he took his hand and put it on top of hers.

Now with tears flowing from her face, Naomi said, "I have longed for this night. I also have waited on you my entire life. I knew the second I saw you, who you were. I was already formed in the sight of God when I met you, but now that you're here with me, I'm whole, and we are now one."

Jeremiah put Naomi into his arms and carried her into the other room. He lightly laid her on the bed. Carefully, he lay next to her and fervently looked into her eyes. He captured her face and pulled it to his! His lips and hers touched! Then they began to passionately kiss! From this point on, everything that was shared between the two that night came naturally. Nervousness and tension where replaced by the desire and the love the two shared for each other.

On this night, a child was conceived. Nine months later Naomi gave birth to their first child, a girl. They name their daughter Ruth, after Jeremiah's mother. In doing this Jeremiah wanted his mother to know that he hadn't forgot about her. Now every time he heard his daughter's name called, he would be reminded of his mother. He wanted his daughter to be a blessing to all she came in contact with, as his mother did.

Having a wife and a child, inspired Jeremiah to give his all when it came to work and providing for his family. Jeremiah's hard work would slowly pay off. Over a course of many years, after the Great Depression, John sold Jeremiah land, were the blacks lived, piece by piece. Jeremiah accumulated a fair amount of land. It was more land than any black person in his area or surrounding areas, had in his lifetime. Although John was kind enough to do this for Jeremiah, no one knew about it until years later. Anyone knowing of John doing this would have caused great problems for himself and for Jeremiah.

Two years after Ruth was born, Naomi gave birth to yet another girl. They named her, Lydia. After having two children, Naomi now appreciated why her mother took such pleasure in being a mother.

Naomi's love for children showed in how quickly her family grew. In 1932, she gave birth to her third child, Sarah. Two years after Sarah was born, Naomi gave birth to her first son, Seth. Jeremiah and Naomi named him after Jeremiah's father. Three years after Seth was born, a second son, James, was born. A year later, finally, the last child was born, Miriam. By 1938, the Strong household was plentiful.

One evening Jeremiah sat and thought of how far he had come; from his lonely life in Kentucky to an entire family in Arkansas. He held great gratitude in his heart for all the things he knew God had given him. Growing from a boy to a man, in an unequal society forced Jeremiah to encounter many storms. All of the storms that he had been through so far hadn't disturbed his faith.

As he sat in his home with his wife, and with his children he knew that this was where he wanted to be. Jeremiah and Naomi's love for each other only grew as the years went on. Both of them instilled in their children the morals and values that they saw suitable, in order for them to do well in life.

Chapter Eight

What the hell do you mean, he's done it before?

Welcome home Floyd ...

A YEAR AFTER MIRIAM WAS born, Naomi went back to teaching. With the additions that Jeremiah had added to their house, there was enough room for more children. One morning after several children had arrived at Naomi's, her sister came to drop of her twin boys, Calvin and Thomas Jr.

"Hey Deb, how are my nephews this fine morning?" asked Naomi.

Deborah didn't respond right away. As she was handing the twins over to Naomi, she held her head down; as if she didn't want Naomi to see her face. Naomi noticed it. She grabbed Deborah by the arm, and attempted to look at her face. "Deb! I asked you a question," said Naomi.

Just then Deborah lifted her head and looked at Naomi, and said, "They're fine!"

Both of Deborah's eyes where nearly closed, they were swollen so. Her lips had been cut on both sides and also swollen. There was large cut of the right side of her head. It was obvious to Naomi that she had been hit in the face.

Very upset over seeing Deborah's face in this condition, Naomi said,

"Deb, stay here, stay here. Let me take the twins in here with the other children. Don't leave!"

All the children were gathered in another room. The oldest of them all was David III. He was the son of Naomi's oldest brother, and his wife Shirley. Naomi said to David III, "Little David, I need you to watch over the smaller children until I finish talking to your Auntie Deb."

"Okay Tee Tee," replied David III.

Naomi hurriedly went back to where Deborah was. She got a cup and poured some water for Deborah. "Here, come sit next to me. What in God's name happened to your face?" asked Naomi.

Deborah sat next to Naomi, embarrassed, with her head hanging down. She began to sob, and replied, "I don't want to talk about it, I'm okay Naomi."

"No, you're not okay! Did Thomas Lee do this to your face?" asked Naomi.

Again, there was not an instant response from Deborah. She looked at Naomi, closed her eyes, and held her head down again. Naomi then put her arm around her and handed her a handkerchief that she had tucked in the waistband of her skirt. In a comforting tone, Naomi said, "Here, take this. Let's get your face cleaned up. You have to tell me who did this. Please Deb, who did this?"

"It was Thomas Lee," said Deborah.

Naomi became visually disturbed over hearing that her brother-in-law did this to her little sister. The same brother-in-law who promised Jessie when he married Deborah, that he wouldn't hurt her granddaughter. Before anyone in the family got married, or even courted, Jessie would be the one to approve or disapprove. When Thomas Lee asked to marry Deborah, Jessie had doubts. Thomas Lee being so persistent aided in Jessie finally saying yes.

"Why, how, could he do this?" asked Naomi.

"He didn't come home the whole weekend. So I asked him this morning when he did show up, where he had been. That made him mad I guess. The next thing I know he was hitting me in the face with his lunch pail. Naomi, I was holding Calvin! We both fell to the floor. I held on to Calvin so he wouldn't hit his head on the floor," said Deborah.

Naomi interrupted and said, "You mean to tell me that he had the nerve to hit you with a pail! He done lost the little mind that the good Lord done gave him. What is the boy's sickness?"

In a somewhat timid manner, Deborah said, "He's done it before, but not this bad. He has never hit me in front of the twins."

Naomi leaped to her feet! "What the hell do you mean, he's done it before? Forgive me Jesus for cussing, but I'm mad now," said Naomi.

Deborah, now shaken by Naomi's reaction, said, "The first time he hit me was before we got married. He told me he was sorry. He didn't do it again until after I got pregnant."

Deborah then stood up next to Naomi, grabbed her arm, and said, "Out of all the times he done hit me, he always said he was sorry. This morning he didn't say it. He spit on me and told me I better not tell anybody that he hit me or he would kill me and the twins."

Thomas Lee's threat to Deborah and the twins infuriated Naomi. "Jesus, you better get him, or I'm going to kill him!" shouted Naomi.

Deborah began to try and calm Naomi, but her efforts were not successful. She then began to plead with Naomi, and said, "Naomi please don't say anything to him. Please don't, I'm begging!"

Naomi sharply turned her head and looked at Deborah! With a very harsh and loud tone, Naomi stated, "Excuse me! You done lost you mind like you're sorry husband! This man said he would kill you and your babies! And you're telling me not to say something! I love Calvin and T.J. more than the amount of fear that Thomas Lee done put in you!"

Deborah sat back down on the couch, held her head down, and continued to sob. She then began to shake her head, and said, "Naomi, I'm scared, and I don't know what to do. I don't want anything to happen to my boys."

Naomi sat down next to Deborah and put her arm around her. She began to console Deborah, and softly said, "Listen Deb, I don't want you to be scared of him. He's not going to hurt you or the twins again. Sit here, I'll be right back."

Naomi went into the room where the kids were. She then told David III, to keep an eye on the kids until her and Deborah returned. She walked back to where Deborah was, snatched her off the couch, and said, "Shut up, don't say a word. It's time for us to have a little talk with Granny!"

Naomi didn't know exactly why she wanted to talk to Jessie. She did feel that Jessie could keep Thomas Lee away from Deborah and the twins. Naomi didn't want to know how or what Jessie would do, but she knew that Jessie would do it.

By this time Jessie was nearly 70 years old. By looking at her, a person couldn't tell her age. She was still vibrant, vocal, and full of hell. When Naomi and Deborah arrived at Jessie's house, she was in the front of the house, talking with William and David Jr. She saw them approaching, but she didn't notice the damage to Deborah's face until they were standing directly in front of her.

Jessie soon noticed Deborah's face before anyone had time to speak. She grabbed Deborah by both arms and pulled her up to her chest, and asked, "Who the hell did this?"

Jessie began shaking Deborah, and shouted, "Look girl, I asked you a damn question?"

Naomi, William, and David Jr. surrounded Jessie and Deborah. They stood there and anxiously waited on Deborah to respond. She didn't respond, so Naomi did, and said, "Granny, Thomas Lee did this to her this morning while she was holding Calvin. This wasn't the first time either."

Jessie, William, and David Jr., were outraged! Jessie released her grip she had on Deborah and stepped back.

"I'm going to kill him!" shouted William.

"You got to get to him first!" exclaimed David Jr.

They both paced the ground, angrily assuring Thomas Lee's death. Jessie, while stomping the ground, and said, "No, no! Hush now. Okay Naomi, who knows about this?"

"Nobody but us Granny, why?" asked Naomi.

Jessie stood in front of Deborah and looked over at Naomi, and shouted, "Girl, you don't ask grown folks why! Are you crazy?"

Jessie then grabbed Deborah by the arms again, looked directly into her eyes, and said, "Dry you face. Stop all this crying and let Granny take care of it. Now, your Uncle Floyd and your brother Jonathan are coming down from Chicago in a couple of days. When they go back, you and your babies are going with them."

At that moment, Deborah tried to speak. Jessie put her hand over Deborah's mouth, and said, "Shut up! You're going to do what I said. Leave everything that you got in that shack. Granny will take care of everything. I might not get things done the right way, but I get them done." Jessie then tightly hugged Deborah.

"Now I told that boy not to hurt you, but he did it anyway. One thing I won't put up with is anybody hurting my girls. I'm tired of telling these hard headed fools that. Do you have a problem with going to Chicago?" asked Jessie.

Deborah still sobbing looked at Jessie and said, "No mam, I will go."

Jessie then instructed Naomi and David Jr. to go and get the twins from Naomi's house. Jessie told all of them standing there not to say anything to anyone about what Thomas Lee had did to Deborah. Naomi and David Jr. left, and William escorted Deborah into Jessie's house.

Two days later, Floyd and Jonathan arrived in New Hope. All the family was glad to see both of them. This was the first time since anyone had seen Floyd since Don had passed away. Floyd was very different from the rest of the family. Wherever there was wrongdoing, Floyd had the front seat. Tales of him fleeing from the police, killing people, as well as robbing people, where always conversation starters, in New Hope's small town gossip scene. Gossip didn't stop anyone in the family from loving Floyd any less. The women in the family had planned a small feast in welcoming home Floyd and Jonathan.

The Other Woman ...

"Hey sugar, how's it going?" asked Thomas Lee.

"Don't ask me how I'm doing. Did anybody see you come in here?" asked Pearline.

"No sugar. It's just you and me tonight," said Thomas Lee.

Pearline grabbed Thomas Lee and embraced him! As she giggled, she asked, "Umm, so where's little Mrs. Perfect? You mean to tell me she let you out on a weekday?"

"She moved out," said Thomas Lee.

Pearline quickly loosened her hold on Thomas Lee, slapped him on the shoulder, and said, "Shut up, you lying!"

Thomas Lee pulled her back up to him, smiled, and said, "No sugar, she did. When I made it home from the weekend, she was not there and I haven't seen her since. Now, you got me all to yourself."

Pearline pushed Thomas Lee back from against her, and in a serious tone, with no smile, she said, "What do you mean she moved out? Please don't think I'm moving in. I got it just fine where I'm at. I don't need nobody being all in love and stuff. I'm damn sure not settling down!"

Thomas Lee became angry and snatched Pearline by her hair, threw her to the floor, and bared his weight on her! Pulling her head back by a hand full of her hair, he said, "What the hell do you mean! You told me you loved me. You said you wanted us to be together!"

Pearline freed herself from Thomas Lee's hold! She jumped to her feet, and ran and grabbed a piece of firewood! Using both hands, she took the piece of wood and came down on Thomas Lee's head! The impact from the wood was so forceful that it caused Thomas Lee to fall to the floor. He was incapable of retaliating.

Pearline stood over Thomas Lee laughing, shaking the piece of firewood over him, and said, "Boy, I don't love you or anybody else for that matter. You was just something to do."

As Pearline stood over Thomas Lee, the front door flew open! Pearline panicked, and said, "Who the hell are you?"

Standing in the doorway was a tall dark black man. She nor Thomas Lee recognized him. "Shut your damn mouth! Who the hell are you?" asked the man.

He slowly walked over to her and Thomas Lee. He raised his hand, holding a pistol, pointed it at Pearline's face, and said, "I'm here for that nigger on the floor. If you rather I talk to you, then so be it!"

Pearline dropped the piece of wood on the floor! She looked at the man, and said, "Look mister, he's all yours." She then dashed off out the door!

Once Pearline dashed out the door, the man stood over Thomas Lee, and pointed the pistol down at his head. With a crooked grin, he cleared his throat, and said, "So I hear you like beating on women and kids, huh? Guess what, I'm what happen to bad ass niggers when they beat on their woman!"

With self arrogance, the man pulled back the trigger and fired one fatal shot into Thomas Lee's head. After he shot Thomas Lee, the man pulled the tip of the pistol up to his mouth and blew it. He then said, "Sorry boy, it had to be done."

The Gathering ...

The evening after Floyd and Jonathan arrived; the family had a small feast at Naomi and Jeremiah's house. Jessie, Bernice, Gertrude, Naomi, and some other women from New Hope, had all prepared dishes for everyone to enjoy. For some, this was their first time meeting Floyd.

The pitter patter of feet from all the children, the smell of soul comforting food, and the stories of the way it use to be, were all in the atmosphere. As everyone there was enjoying the food and the environment, Jeremiah noticed that Deborah, Thomas Lee, or the twins were not there. "Where's Deb them? I haven't seen her Thomas Lee, or the twins this evening," said Jeremiah.

Just as Jeremiah asked about Deborah, he noticed Jessie inconspicuously hitting Naomi on the arm. He also noticed the two women along with Floyd, William, and David Jr. all looked at one another after he asked about Deborah. He didn't think anything of it, he just stood there and waited on anyone to respond.

Gertrude, having not seen any of them, responded, "I don't know. Come to think of it, I haven't seen them all day."

"More than likely the twins done wore them out. They'll get to see Floyd and Jonathan before they leave out for Chicago tomorrow," said Naomi.

Everyone continued to enjoy the rest of the evening. A little while later into the evening, as everyone talked, Jessie and Floyd excused themselves and walked outside. Jeremiah noticed the two of them leaving. Before everyone left for the evening, he wanted to talk to Floyd before he left. Getting to know Floyd was important to Jeremiah. He knew all of Naomi's family except Floyd.

Jessie and Floyd had been outside for over an hour. Jeremiah decided to walk outside to see if they had left. Once he made it outside, he didn't see them. He heard voices coming from the back of the house. He started to say something, but he stopped in his tracks after hearing Thomas Lee's name. He eased a little closer to the voices, when he realized that it was Jessie and Floyd.

Boastfully laughing, Floyd went on to say, "Oh no, don't worry about that. I was quicker than the other three."

"You better be sure it's done. I'm getting so tired of these fools coming in this family and hurting my girls. Here, take this! It'll be enough to help her and them youngins," said Jessie.

Jeremiah saw Jessie hand something to Floyd. The two then turned to walk towards the front of the house. Just as they turned around, Jeremiah ran back inside. He forgot about wanting to talk to Floyd.

After he made it back inside, Jeremiah saw that everyone was preparing to leave. Him and Naomi saw everyone out the door. After straightening up some, they went to lie down for the night. The piece of conversation that Jeremiah overheard bothered him. He didn't know what Jessie and Floyd where talking about, but he felt in his spirit that it wasn't anything descent.

Jeremiah rolled over in the bed and faced Naomi, and asked, "Naomi, are you sleep?"

"No, I'm not sleep. Why, is everything okay?" asked Naomi.

"Well I'm not sure. I overheard Jessie and Floyd talking around back, but they didn't see me," said Jeremiah.

Naomi rose up and propped her hand underneath her face. She became nervous about what Jeremiah may have heard. "You did! What were they saying?" asked Naomi.

"Well before I got to close, I heard them say Thomas Lee's name. Then as I got a little closer, I heard Floyd laughing. He said something like, 'Don't worry about that. It was quicker than the other three.' Then I think Jessie said something to the sort of, 'I'm tired of fools coming in this family and hurting my girls.' Then she handed him something and said, 'Take this, it'll be enough for her and them youngins.' Do you have an idea what they could have been talking about?" asked Jeremiah.

Naomi sat up in the bed, and said, "I think I need to tell you something."

Jeremiah sat upright in the bed as well, and said, "Go ahead, I'm listening."

Naomi began to put pieces of her past together with what Jeremiah said that he overheard. She recalled her and Jessie's conversation about her father, Alecta, and Alecta's mom and brother.

A few years before I met you, I met a girl on a church trip. After me and her finished talking, we had made plans for her, her mother, and her brother to come up for the weekend. Anyway, they never showed up. To make a long story short, a few years after that, their church visited our church. A girl that remembered me told me that all three of them had been killed," said Naomi.

Jeremiah suddenly interrupted Naomi and said, "Oh my goodness!"

"Yes, they were all killed, but that's not all of it. After talking to the girl about them being killed, I put two and two together and figured out that Daddy was fooling around with the woman that got killed, Mary Ann. The two kids she had that got killed, were Daddy's," said Naomi.

Jeremiah was stunned. "You have got to be fooling." said Jeremiah.

"No, I wish I was. I and Granny, besides Daddy, are the only ones who knew about his other family. When I figured it out, I wanted to tell Momma, but Granny wasn't hearing that. She told me I had better keep my mouth shut. The same thing you heard her say was the same thing she said back then, 'no body better not hurt my girls.' She scared me so I never said anything to anybody about it," said Naomi.

"Well, do you think she had something to do with it?" asked Jeremiah.

"I'm not sure what to think when it comes to Granny. I don't want to think that she could do something so evil. On the other hand, the things she said then, and the things you said that she said tonight, make me wonder. I'm beginning to wonder if Thomas Lee is even alive," said Naomi.

"Why do you say that?" asked Jeremiah.

"A couple of days ago, Deb came to drop the twins off. She was all swollen and beat up, pretty bad. Of course she said that Thomas Lee had done it. So I got mad and told Granny. I didn't know what else to do. Deb was really scared because he told her that he was going to kill her and the twins if she told anybody. After we finished talking to Granny, she told us not to say anything to nobody about Deb getting beat up. Then she hid Deb and twins out at her house. She did tell us that she would take care of it," said Naomi.

"Why didn't you tell me?" asked Jeremiah.

"I don't know. I was so mad, I just wanted him to pay for what he did to my sister," said Naomi.

"So what, are Deb and the twins going back to Chicago with Floyd?" asked Jeremiah.

"Yea, they're supposed to be leaving tomorrow," said Naomi.

"Okay, but where Thomas Lee is?" asked Jeremiah.

"I don't know. Granny said she'll take care of it, I don't want to know how she's going to take care of it," said Naomi.

"I'm going to go look for him first thing in the morning. I pray that I find him, alive. I know what he did was wrong, but I could have talked to him or we could have got the police involved," said Jeremiah.

"You know what? The girl that told me how Alecta them got killed, told me they arrested somebody. She said that the neighbor saw a man and a woman go into their house the night before they were found dead."

"Then the man said that the man they arrested was not the same man he saw and that nobody else went into that house. I'm thinking now, that maybe some kind of way, Uncle Floyd killed them for Granny," said Naomi.

"I don't know Naomi. I know she's mean and conniving, but I don't think she could have a child killed," said Jeremiah.

"You're right. Let's just pray about it and we'll both check on Thomas Lee tomorrow," said Naomi.

Jeremiah then kissed Naomi goodnight and they both lay down to sleep. After their discussion, the last thing on their minds was sleep. Naomi thought she would never be happy to see Thomas Lee, but she desperately wanted to see him the next day.

Chapter Nine

*Granny, Jeremiah and them found Thomas
Lee shot to death this morning.*

We found Thomas Lee ...

Early the next morning, Jeremiah arose, intent on finding Thomas
Lee. He told Naomi to stay home with the children. After he left home
he stopped by Ronnie's house to get him to go with him in search of
Thomas Lee. The two men headed towards Deborah and Thomas Lee's
house. As they were walking, they met up with Harold and Kent; they
were on their way to work.

Jeremiah told Kent and Harold where he and Ronnie were going.
As they walked, Jeremiah filled the men in on what he and Naomi
had talked about the night before. Once Jeremiah finished talking and
just before they made it to Thomas Lee's house, Kent stopped in his
tracks!

"Hey man, what's wrong? Why did you stop?" asked Jeremiah.

Kent hesitated to tell Jeremiah what he was thinking, but he told
him anyway. "Hey, Jay, I wasn't gone say nothing, but I got too. I was
on the Hill last night, getting a good snoot full. Pearline came running
up on everybody, real quick like. She was breathing all hard and stuff.
Bud asked her what was going on. She said that she was at home with
Thomas Lee and this man busted in with a gun. She said he told her he

68

wanted Thomas Lee, not her. So she said she took off down to the Hill where we was all at," said Kent.

"Was she talking about Deb's Thomas Lee?" asked Jeremiah.

"Man you know it's only one Thomas Lee in these here parts. Yeah, it's the same one! Everybody in town knows who Pearline be fooling with," said Kent.

"Yeah Jay, everybody know," said Harold.

"Everybody doesn't know! Did she know who the man was?" asked Jeremiah.

"Nope, she said he was tall and black and had a pistol. After she put down a couple snoots, she said she was leaving New Hope and going to stay with her folks further south," said Kent.

The four men continued to walk. Jeremiah asked Kent, "Do you know where she lives?"

"Yeah, I know. Why?" asked Kent.

"Well nobody has seen him in a few days. If he's not at home, we're going to check by Pearline house," said Jeremiah.

The men arrived at Thomas Lee's house. They went inside, but no one was there. They then headed towards Pearline's house, with Kent leading the way. As they approached her house, they noticed the door was opened. Once inside they discovered Thomas Lee's dead body on the floor!

It was shocking for them to see him laying there on the floor dead, with a bullet hole in his head. Ronnie agreed to stay with the body, while Kent and Harold went to get help. Jeremiah ran to tell the family. Upon arriving home, he learned from Naomi that Floyd, Jonathan, Deborah, and her twins had left for Chicago.

After Jeremiah informed Naomi that they had found Thomas Lee dead at Pearline's house, she became upset. For the second time she wondered if Jessie was capable of killing someone. Jeremiah proceeded to tell her of the conversation that he had just had with his friends. Naomi was disgusted over hearing the news that Thomas Lee had been cheating on Deborah. It reminded her of her own father cheating on her mother.

Jeremiah told Naomi that he was going to go talk with Jessie. "Why are you going to talk to Granny?" asked Naomi.

"I need to know if she or your Uncle Floyd knows anything about

Thomas Lee being shot. Could this be what they were talking about last night?" asked Jeremiah.

"I'm not sure, but I'm going with you. Ruth can watch the smaller kids," said Naomi.

Jeremiah and Naomi headed off to Jessie's house. Once they made it there, she greeted them at the door, and said, "Morning."

"Morning Granny," said both Jeremiah and Naomi.

"What brings yall here this early in the morning?" asked Jessie. She walked back over to where she had been sitting and continued to knit.

"Granny, Jeremiah and them found Thomas Lee shot to death this morning," said Naomi.

Jessie continued knitting and nonchalantly said, "Oh my, that's too bad for him."

Both Jeremiah and Naomi were bothered over Jessie's non caring attitude. "Granny, don't you think Deb needs to know?" asked Naomi.

Jessie stopped knitting and looked over at Naomi, and said, "Why do she need to know? She got enough to worry bout her own self, without being bothered with this mess!" Jessie then started back knitting and began quietly humming to herself.

Jeremiah and Naomi exchanged looks and were both in disbelief. Then Jeremiah said to Jessie, "Granny I know you probably didn't like Thomas Lee, but he still was a child of God. It's not our place to pass judgment against him. God is the one who suppose to do the judging."

Jessie stopped knitting again. She became very distressed and said, "God, God, God, that's all you talk about! Where was your God when Thomas Lee was beating my grandbaby upside the head? Some things you have to take care of yourself. Now, you two have wasted enough of my time, coming all the way here to tell me about that boy. I don't care today and I damn sure won't care tomorrow! If that's all," said Jessie. She then started to knit again and continued humming quietly.

Jeremiah and Naomi where both speechless. They took Jessie's comments as a sign to leave. As they started to leave out the door, Jessie said, "Oh, by the way Mr. Preacher man, don't you go getting any ideas. Thomas Lee wasn't the first man to ever get shot in the head, and sure won't be the last. I don't care what it takes; nobody is going to hurt my girls. Now you kids have a nice day." It became obvious to both Jeremiah and Naomi that they weren't going to get anywhere with talking to Jessie.

Thomas Lee was eventually laid to rest. As the years went on the rumors of who done it and why slowly faded into to the background. His death was never investigated. The sheriff of the county lived 20 miles away, and was heard to have said, 'that's one less nigger we got to worry about.'

A year after Deborah had been in Chicago, the thought of Thomas Lee never entered her mind. She sent word to Naomi to let her know that her and the twins where doing well. Naomi informed their mother Bernice, along with all the other family members, of Deborah's well being.

Chicago wasn't absent from racial issues or economic struggles, but it provided more opportunities for black Americans. By the time Deborah had arrived in Chicago in 1939, many black Chicagoans were paving the way for equality.

Things weren't evolving nearly as frequently in the south as they were in the north. The Strongs were content with their environment. Their environment had many faults, but it could have been worse. There were many counties in Arkansas that didn't allow blacks at all.

Jeremiah considered such discrimination as hatred. He viewed hatred as evil. Having Bill as a boss, instead of as a master, meant a lot to the Strong family. Bill was often scrutinized by his white peers for his belief in equality. He hired black workers in a time when it was hard for any race to be employed. Although Bill's white peers scrutinized him, they didn't dare act on their feelings.

Bill and his family were one of the wealthiest families in the south. Alone, Bill funded a small church based school for black children. All of the children that were previously taught by Naomi attended the school. The school was functional until the mid 1950s.

Once Naomi started teaching school at the church, she had a few more books, but the same amount of children that she had when she taught out of her house. As Naomi's children grew, she began to see the potential they had; especially the two oldest children, Ruth and Lydia. Naomi had previously been attentive to how the two girls had excelled the books that she had.

In the late 1940s, Naomi received a letter from Deborah. After Naomi had read the letter, she wanted Jeremiah to read it as will. He sat down and begun to read the letter, saying, " 'My dear sister. How are you and your family? I hope all is well with you. Me and the twins are doing well. They are both in school and really learning a lot. I'm now working at a hospital here. Can you believe they actually have a hospital for black folks here! Anyway, the main reason I'm writing you is about Ruth and Lydia. I know how smart they are. It's more chances here for them to go to college. The Pastor of my church and some of the members, have set up a small scholarship fund for black children. It's for black children who are serious about learning. The harder the child works, the more help they can get. I talked to them' 'about Ruth and Lydia and they want them to come here and be tested. Naomi this is a chance of a lifetime for them. Could you and Jeremiah please consider letting them come.' "

After Jeremiah had finished reading the letter, he and Naomi discussed what Deborah had said in the letter. After much debating, they both talked with Ruth and Lydia. Both girls were ecstatic! In 1947 Deborah and her new husband, Andrew, traveled to Arkansas to get Ruth and Lydia.

Once they arrived back to Chicago, both girls took the required test. Ruth was the first person to have taken the test to get a perfect score. She soon began college. Lydia, who was only 16, missed one question. Both of the girl's intelligence impressed the scholarship board members. A year after Ruth had begun college, Lydia began. Both girls exceeded in every area in which they studied.

Naomi and Jeremiah received a letter from the girls every other week. Naomi and Jeremiah saw that their decision to let the girls go to Chicago was a good decision.

Chapter Ten

Naomi, kids, this is my cousin Wilton, from Kentucky

Something from the Past ...

Two years after Ruth and Lydia had left Arkansas; the Strong's received a knock on the front door. It was a Sunday morning in 1949; the Strong's were preparing for breakfast. The aroma of homemade biscuits and the sizzling sound of dry salt meat filled the air.

You could tell it was Sunday in the Strong house by the smell of dry salt meat. Naomi had a specific meat for each day of the week; Sunday was Miriam and Jeremiah's favorite day of the week. Miriam was the first one in the kitchen. "Momma can I help you do something?" asked Miriam

Whenever Naomi was in the kitchen cooking, Miriam would always run in to see if she could help. "Sure Miry, you can get a spoon and put butter in the biscuits for Momma," replied Naomi.

Miriam couldn't get to the butter fast enough! One of her favorite things in the world was to sit and look at Naomi cook. Whenever she would let Miriam help, her entire face would light up.

As Naomi finished preparing breakfast, you could hear everyone in the house moving around, getting ready for breakfast. Jeremiah was the first one to come into the kitchen. He walked over to Miriam with both of his arms opened. She leaped into his arms! They sat down at the table. With a coy smile on his face, Jeremiah said, "Are you helping Momma Miry or getting in the way?"

"I'm putting butter in the biscuits Daddy," said Miriam.

Jeremiah leaned in and whispered in Miriam's ear, saying, "Did you put extra butter in mine?"

In a whisper, Miriam replied, "Yes sir, don't I always."

The rest of the Strong family came in to join the others for breakfast. After they were all seated, Jeremiah's words, every time they sat down to eat: "Heads down, eyes closed, and hands together." Jeremiah blessed every piece of food that entered their home.

As Jeremiah closed the prayer, it was a knock at the front door. He got up to answer the door and instructed his family to continue eating. While sitting at the table, Miriam focused on the fact that she had only one piece of dry salt meat, while the others were looking towards the front door. Curiosity got the best of Naomi, so she asked Jeremiah, "Who's at the door?"

"Nobody," he replied. At the same time he was pushing the visitor out the door. Jeremiah then said, "Naomi, I'll be right back."

Naomi sat there in confusion along with her children. They saw a man at the door, but they didn't know why Jeremiah said that nobody was there. "Momma, who is that man," asked Seth.

"I don't know sweetie, I never seen him around here before," said Naomi.

A few minutes later, Jeremiah and the man went back inside the house. Jeremiah didn't have a content look on his face. His demeanor and presence was different. "Naomi, kids, this is my cousin Wilton, from Kentucky," said Jeremiah.

Jeremiah began introducing his family one at a time to Wilton. "This here is Seth, my oldest boy. This is James, my youngest boy. This is Sarah, my third oldest, and this little one is Miriam, but we call her Miry," said Jeremiah.

"Jeremiah you never told me that you had any family left living," said Naomi.

"I know baby, I didn't because Wilton here, left Kentucky when I was a young boy. I didn't know what happened to him. We all thought he was dead somewhere," said Jeremiah.

"But I'm not dead cousin Jay. I know I can't make up for lost times, but I do want to at least try, if you'll let me," said Wilton.

"Kids yall help Momma straighten up the kitchen," said Jeremiah.

"But Daddy we want to talk to Wilton," said James.

Jeremiah softly tapped James on the bottom, and said, "Boy do as I said. Me and Wilton are going to step outside and talk for a minute."

Jeremiah and Wilton walked around back to the smoke house that Jeremiah had built. Once the two men were inside the smoke house, they sat down to talk. Jeremiah sat in disbelief on seeing Wilton again. Once Wilton left after his mother, Ruth, died, he thought he would never see Wilton again.

Jeremiah began the conversation, and said, "Wilton, what are you doing here? How did you know how to find me?"

"Well Jay, I went back to our home town and everyone was just about gone. I asked around and was told that you had moved here," said Wilton.

For a brief second, Jeremiah simply looked at Wilton. He was amazed to see how aged Wilton appeared. He was only 40 years old, but to Jeremiah he looked to be 60. Jeremiah then said, "You know Wilton, you got a lot of nerve showing your face to me after what you did."

Wilton stood up and said, "Look Jay, I wanted to stick around, but the heat was getting hot."

Jeremiah looked up at Wilton, and said, "Oh, so the heat was getting hot, huh. Tell me Wilton, how was the heat to hot for you. My momma was killed, your own auntie! You were the only family I had left! And you mean to tell me the heat was too hot!"

Jeremiah held his head down, placed his hands together, and began to cry. Wilton walked over to him, kneeled down, and placed his hand on Jeremiah's knee, and said, "I'm sorry Jay! I know that don't mean much, but I am. It was so much commotion going on when Tee Tee died. You remember Dale's daughter I was messing around with?" asked Wilton.

"Yeah, why?" asked Jeremiah.

"She told me she overheard Dale, Marvin, and LeCester say that I did it," said Wilton.

Jeremiah stood up! "What are you talking about?" asked Jeremiah.

"The night they found Tee Tee, she said that her momma sent her out to get some wood. She said she heard some voices coming from behind the house. Dale and the others were standing by the burn barrel.

They didn't see her. She got close enough to hear them. Marvin said that he and LeCester saw me. They said I must have done it," said Wilton.

This was the first Jeremiah had heard this. He then replied, "Well LeCester and Marvin told the two men from the E.R.O.C.P what they saw when they found Momma. Not one time did they say you killed Momma? Now, it was all kind of rumors, but I never heard this one."

"What do you mean, E.R.O.C.P?" asked Wilton.

"It's some type of outfit that helps the families of black people who get killed. They kind of like police, they find out who did it. So, they talked to all of us. Marvin and LeCester said that they thought it was you they saw, but it couldn't have been, because the man they saw didn't answer them. If I would have thought you had anything to do with it, I would have known," said Jeremiah.

"Well, this E.R.O.C.P, did they find out who did it?" asked Wilton.

"No. As of a few years ago they hadn't. They sent me a letter and told me that whoever killed Momma was the same person who had killed seven women and a young girl," said Jeremiah.

"What, I never heard of them," said Jeremiah.

"Well they good people. They took the dress Momma had on and the rock that was lying next to her head," said Jeremiah.

"Why did they do that?" asked Wilton.

"They said that they were going to compare it to stuff from their other cases. They got some pretty smart people that work with them. One day, if it's the Lord's will, they'll find out who did it," said Jeremiah.

"Wow!" said Wilton.

"I tell you what Wilton, the day you came running up to me and told me Momma was dead, I got sick man. The way she died, man a dog didn't deserve that. Momma never hurt anybody," said Jeremiah.

The memories of his mother dying were taking Jeremiah to a place he didn't want to be. He then said, "Wilton that's in the past now and that's where I want to leave it. I don't want my family getting all upset about it. I'll tell them when I'm ready," said Jeremiah.

Wilton and Jeremiah finally hugged. Wilton then looked Jeremiah in the eyes and said, "Fine with me Jay. I won't say nothing." He then began to cry and went on to say, "Jay, will you please forgive me for leaving you? I'm so sorry man."

Jeremiah grabbed both sides of Wilton's face and said, "I forgave you a long time ago. You need to forgive yourself."

Jeremiah hadn't held a grudge against Wilton for leaving him alone. His loneliness was replaced with the words of God. His sorrow had only made him stronger. That day he knew that he had to tell Naomi about his past.

After Jeremiah and Wilton finished talking alone, they went back into the house. Naomi had fixed Wilton a plate of food. "Wilton, here I fixed you a plate. Come sit down at the table and eat. Kids, keep Wilton company while me and Daddy go into the other room and talk," said Naomi.

All the children ran over to where Wilton was, to get to know him a little better. Jeremiah walked over to Naomi and took her by the hand, and led her into the other room.

Once the two were in the other room, Naomi sat on the bed, while Jeremiah kneeled at her knees. He then took Naomi by both her hands and gave them a soft kiss.

"So Jeremiah, why have I never heard of Wilton?" asked Naomi.

Jeremiah took a deep breath and released it. This is the day he had never wanted to see come. Jeremiah never wanted the dark part of his past to encounter the light of his future; which was his family.

"Well Naomi, Wilton is my cousin. He's Momma's nephew. I didn't tell you about him because he's from a time in my life I didn't want to remember," said Jeremiah.

Naomi took her hand and lovingly caressed the side of Jeremiah's face, and said, "Jeremiah I am your wife and those are your children in the next room. Don't you think we need to know where you came from; good or bad? Keeping things hid, as you can see, leads to a unexpected knock on the door years later. Don't you love us enough to share your past with us?"

"Look Naomi, it's not that I don't love yall, I do love you, so much that it hurts sometimes. If the thought enters my mind that something can hurt you, it rips me up inside," said Jeremiah. Jeremiah, now with tears falling from his eyes, took a hold of Naomi's hands and lowered his head.

"Baby, are you okay?" asked Naomi.

"Yeah I'm okay. I just didn't know this day would come," said Jeremiah.

"I know it's hard. Just take your time. Things left unsaid are harder to bear than things we confess," said Naomi.

"Wilton's daddy, my Uncle Joe, was killed when Wilton was a boy. Momma took him into her house as her own son. Wilton and I were real close. When I was 17, my Momma was killed. That left me and him," said Jeremiah.

Naomi in a state of shock, said, "Jeremiah, my goodness, I'm so sorry!"

"I know baby. It's not just that she was killed, it was the way she was killed," said Jeremiah.

"How?" asked Naomi.

The forgotten visions of Ruth's body had just reentered Jeremiah's memory. It deeply saddened him. He then said, "She was raped! She was beaten! She was left naked, like she was a dog!"

Naomi tried to desperately reassure Jeremiah that everything was okay. She reached out and hugged Jeremiah. She held him tight and rubbed his back, and said, "It's okay baby, it's okay."

Jeremiah pulled himself back from Naomi, while holding her hands in his. He sat her back down on the bed. "I know baby. I just hate that I wasn't there to protect her. She was all alone," said Jeremiah.

Naomi grabbed Jeremiah by both shoulders, shook him, and said, "Stop it! Don't blame yourself. What do you say all the time to me and the kids? 'God has a purpose for everything that happens.' I know it's hard to think of her being killed like that, but it had to have a purpose, don't it?" asked Naomi.

Jeremiah gathered his composure as well as he could, and said, "I know that God has a purpose for everything, I have never questioned why she had to die. Talking about it doesn't make it any easier."

"So let's not talk about her death anymore. I see why it's hard for you to talk about it. So, back to Wilton," said Naomi.

"Well after Momma was killed, two men from a outfit called the E.R.O.C.P, came to look into her death. They help the families of black people who get killed. They talked to the two men who found Momma's body. They wanted to talk to Wilton, but he had left town. He just told me outside he left town because he heard people was saying that he had killed Momma," said Jeremiah.

"Oh my Jeremiah, why would somebody say such a thing?" asked Naomi.

"It was bunches of here say, what it was. He had always left town before Momma had died. He just didn't want to hear people talking about him. I told him I never heard anybody say that. I did get a letter a while ago from the E.R.O.C.P. They hadn't found out who did it, but whoever did it was the same person who had killed seven other women and a young girl," said Jeremiah.

"Good Lord, that's awful. Who would do something like that?" asked Naomi.

"A monster, it had to be! One of these days they'll find out who did it. I pray to God everyday that whoever killed Momma and the other women, will be caught," said Jeremiah.

"They will baby. The word says, 'Therefore judge nothing before the time, until the Lord comes, who will bring to light the hidden things of darkness and reveal the counsels of the heart.' So Jeremiah, the sins of whoever did this to Momma Ruth and the other women, will be brought to light by God, in his time," said Naomi.

Naomi then grabbed both sides of Jeremiah's cheeks, wiped his tears with the tips of her thumbs, and kissed him on the lips, and said, "Close your eyes."

Jeremiah placed both his hands on top of Naomi's hands, tenderly kissed her hand, and closed his eyes.

Naomi closed her eyes and held her head down, and said, "Lord, let your will be done in the situation concerning Momma Ruth. Lord God, bless our family with the strength to bare this heavy burden. Lord we know that you are God of all comfort. Your word says that you comfort us in all our tribulations. We come to you now Lord seeking strength, patience, and comfort. Lord will you help us to keep our minds stayed on you. In Jesus' name do we pray for these things? Amen."

Naomi and Jeremiah stood there holding each other. Jeremiah's tears had dried. He then smiled at Naomi, and said, "You are an amazing woman Naomi Strong."

"Same to you, Mr. Jeremiah Strong. Okay, so what about Wilton? Is he staying, going, what?" asked Naomi.

"Well he wants to stay, so I'm going to talk to Mr. Bill about hiring him on. He needs an extra hand, so he probably will. A couple of those shacks he got left standing by the fields are empty. So, we'll see," said Jeremiah.

"That's fine. It'll all work out for the best," said Naomi.

Later on this day, Jeremiah took Wilton to see Bill Mathews. Bill hired Wilton and let him live in one of the shacks, on Jeremiah's word that Wilton would work.

Naomi didn't tell Jeremiah that she had an unsettling feeling about his cousin Wilton. She took the feeling she had as the fact he was a stranger to her and to their children.

Wilton started working, he proved to be very dependable. When not working, Wilton mostly stayed to himself. Jeremiah noticed that he was much different than when they were younger. When Wilton was younger, he was loud, outgoing, and sought trouble. Now, much older, he had calmed.

Wilton was later introduced to Naomi's family. He was glad to see familiar faces; Kent, Ronnie, and Harold. Their families had grown since Wilton last saw them back in Kentucky. Kent was now married to Leah, William and Gertrude's daughter. They had four children. Only their youngest child, Ruby, still lived in New Hope.

Ronnie and Lucille had two children. Now adults, the children had left New Hope and relocated in Little Rock, Arkansas. Ronnie and Lucille spent most of their free time with their small circle of friends.

Harold and Lillie were no longer together. Lillie had moved to another county farther south. Their children were grown and had children of their own. Harold was now remarried to a local woman, Onnie. They had two children of their own.

As with Ronnie, Lucille, Kent, and Leah, Harold and Onnie spent their free time with their small familiar circle of friends. Everyone welcomed Wilton with open arms to their community. So Wilton didn't feel alone, because he was surrounded by people he knew and also Jeremiah's extended family.

Chapter Eleven

In a moment of excitement both girls leaped up, holding hands, they danced around their new dollhouses.

Greatest Gift Ever ...

A YEAR AFTER WILTON HAD been in Arkansas, all was well in his life. He had worked for Bill the entire year without missing a day. As far as a social life, he didn't really have one. He mostly stayed to himself. Out of courtesy, Naomi would send him a plate of food on Sundays, by Miriam and Ruby. Receiving the warm plates of food made Wilton feel loved by Jeremiah and his family.

Ruth and Miriam were both now 12 years old. Just like their mothers, Naomi and Leah, they were best friends. Other than at home, neither of the two girls was seen without the other. Six months after Miriam and Ruby had been taking Wilton his Sunday plates, he invited them inside. Before entering the house Miriam observed how dark it was inside.

"Cousin Wilton, will you make it brighter in here, it's too dark?" asked Naomi.

"Oh sure Miry. I'm sorry girls, it's just me here, so I keep it dark," said Wilton.

Wilton walked over and took down the dark fabric he had up to the window blocking the sunlight from shining through. The light from the sun lit the entire room.

"You girls sit there. I made something for you, for being so nice and bringing me this warm food all this time. I'll be right back," said Wilton.

Miriam and Ruby sat there giggling with anticipation on what Wilton had made for them. Both girls knew that Wilton was very skillful with making things out of wood. He made all types of beautiful furniture and toys. Not only did the local people by his wood work, people from different counties did as well, both black and white people. So Miriam figured that he had made them something out of wood. She just hoped it wasn't furniture.

Wilton walked back over to where the girls were and handed them each a wooden dollhouse. Miriam thought to herself that her dollhouse was the prettiest thing she had ever seen. Both girls were elated.

"Cousin Wilton, it's so pretty! Thank you, thank you!" said Miriam.

Ruby, being equally excited, and said, "Cousin Wilton, how did you make something like this? They are so pretty."

In a moment of excitement both girls leaped up, holding hands, they danced around their new dollhouses. Then they ran and gave Wilton hugs of appreciation. "Well girls, that's what I like to do with my spare time. I knew yall would get a kick out of them. I didn't know you would like them this much. I'm glad you like them," said Wilton.

"Ruby, let's go so we can put our babies in them," said Naomi.

"Okay! This is going to be so much fun. Wait until everybody sees them," said Ruby.

"You girls don't have to leave. You are more than welcome to play with them here, if you'd like," said Wilton.

Miriam ran over and gave Wilton another hug, kissed him on the cheek, and said, "We're going to take them home and play with them. Plus we want to show them off."

"Okay girls, yall be careful taking them home and get those babies in them so they'll have a home of their own," said Wilton.

Wilton saw the girls off and waved good-bye. The feelings of excitement couldn't be measured for Miriam and Ruby. They showed their dollhouses off to everybody. Naomi and Jeremiah were impressed with the effort that Wilton had put into the dollhouses.

Later Naomi had Jessie to make both of the girls' new dolls to go with their new dollhouses. Jeremiah would have to pick Miriam up off the floor at night, because she would fall asleep playing with her dollhouse.

Over the next few weeks Miriam and Ruby, as well as the other black people in their town, readied for the black county fair. The fair was the biggest attraction for the local blacks. This was the time for everyone to get together, play games, listen to local singers, and enjoy a feast of different foods.

Miriam and Ruby had been preparing for the county fair. They both had helped Jessie make quilts to sell at the fair. On the day of the fair, Jessie had Miriam and Ruby to come to her house to help her pack up the quilts to be sold.

Once they arrived at the carnival they enjoyed how pretty everything was. The local black people, as well as blacks from neighboring towns, flocked to enjoy the events of the fair. Miriam and Ruby spent most of their time, helping Jessie at her stand. Jessie soon gave the girls permission to go off and enjoy the festivities offered at the fair.

This was music to their young ears. Miriam and Ruby dashed off to join in on the festivities and eat as much junk food as possible. As the day began to come to a end, Ruby was called by her mother to help her carry some things home. She told Miriam that she would be back in a little while. After Ruby returned, she looked for Miriam, but because of all the excitement of the day, no one had noticed that she wasn't there.

Chapter Twelve

No! Miriam recognized the face of the voice!

Miriam's Demon ...

"Why am I here? It's so dark. I need to find my out of here," said Miriam

Miriam reached her hands out in front of her to feel her unseen surroundings. She stood to her feet to take a step, she fell to the floor! The darkness was so dark that it was thick. Miriam couldn't see, but she felt that something was binding her feet together. She reached down to loosen the bind from her feet. As she struggled to loosen the bind, the faint sounds of footsteps were getting closer. After hearing the footsteps, Miriam began to desperately try to free herself. Just as she began making process, she saw a narrow beam of light coming through a door.

Now petrified, Miriam shouted, "Who's there? Pleading and now weeping, she begged, "Please say something!" Miriam felt that she was in an unfamiliar situation, but she couldn't remember how she got there or where she was.

"Shhhh," he whispered.

Cradling her body while she sat on the floor, Miriam asked, "Where am I? Who are you?"

In a low sinister voice, he replied, "It's okay. You fell asleep at the fair and I brought you here so you could sleep."

His voice and his statement frightened Miriam even more. She began to cry uncontrollably, and said, "I don't want to be here. I want to go home to my Momma."

She began begging the demon to let her go! "Please, please let me go home. My Momma and Daddy are going to be worried."

Like a slithering snake on the prowl for innocent prey, the man eased over to Miriam. He reached down and grabbed her! He slammed her to the floor! Just as she hit the floor, the narrow beam of light from the door became wider. The light shinned directly onto the demon's face.

No! Miriam recognized the face of the voice! She started to speak, saying, "But why are you ...

Before Miriam could get another word out of her mouth, he covered it. Now with his hand over her mouth, his body crushing hers, he bent down to her ear, and said, "Shut up! Don't make this any harder than it has to be little girl. Don't you say one word, I mean it! Lay here and don't move!"

Miriam did as he said. She couldn't believe that the man was being so mean and hurting her. She didn't know what he was doing to her or why he was doing it. But she knew that she was afraid. She didn't see him as a man anymore; he became a demon in Miriam's mind.

His hand was so large and heavy covering Miriam's mouth, it was hard for her to breath. She lay there motionless with her eyes closed. She took herself out of the grips of the demon in her mind. Mentally she was sitting in the field next to her house, laughing and playing with Ruby. 'Where are you Ruby? Ruby, please come to me.'

The demon became immorally aroused from Miriam's fear and her inability to move. She was no longer a little girl to him, she was his prey. He had his prey exactly where he wanted it. As a hunter would, he had stalked, set a trap, and patiently waited for his prey to arrive into in captivity.

With his free hand, he reached under Miriam's dress and snatched it over her head. As if he was ripping paper, he ripped her underwear from her body. The touch of Miriam's bare body was disgustingly satisfying the horrendous sexual appetite of the demon.

Getting inside of the innocence and purity of his prey was inevitable. Days and months had gone by with him resisting raping the innocence and purity of his prey. In his sick battle of resistance versus rape, resistance had just lost.

He took his producer of life and forced it into Miriam's virginity! She screamed! Her screams were unheard. The demon doggedly forced his way into her over and over. Harder than each time before. The pain was excessive for Miriam. Her body now covered in her own blood. As he continued, the sweat from his head trickled down onto her face.

Her body, her thoughts, and her sense of being were now numb. They had all been stolen by the demon's wicked desires. Once His Needs, had been met, his prey laid there on the floor, paralyzed. The things that she lost this night were now his gains. He was gratified with his victory. Once again, he had won in robbing the innocence of defenseless prey.

He stood over Miriam's bare, beaten, and bloody body with a bucket of hot water. He dashed her body with the water; trying to cleanse any evidence of his transgression. Although he washed away all of his damage on the outside of her body, the inside he couldn't clean. Miriam's cerebral status was no more. She hadn't any thoughts. Her heart was deeply saddened.

Once the demon had washed, dried, and dressed her, she stood there in hell, completely absent from reality. The demon gently (in his knowing) took Miriam by the hand and led her from hell. As she got ready to leave off into the sunlight, he stopped her. He kneeled down to her level, with a cowardly smile on his face, and said, "I didn't mean to hurt you Miry. It always hurts the first time. Don't worry, the next time it won't hurt so bad. Make sure you don't tell anybody what we did together. Some things even grown folks don't understand. If you're Momma or Daddy found out, they would just die. You don't want anything to happen to them, do you?"

He then reached into the pocket of his paints and pulled something out. He handed it to Miriam, and said, "Here, take this pretty necklace. Take care of it because it belonged to somebody close to me. I want you to come back and see me in three days. If you don't then something really, really, bad will happen to your pretty little Momma, okay," said the demon.

Miriam didn't answer him fast enough, so the demon took her by both of her shoulders and shook her, saying, "Did you hear me!"

His tone and the strength of his voice triggered Miriam's absent mental capability. Frightened, Miriam nodded her head in agreement with the demon. He then stood up, rubbed her on the head, and said, "Good girl. Now get home before your Momma and Daddy get worried!"

Miriam No Longer Speaks ...

Miriam's body had been greatly damaged. She was hurt and confused. She didn't know why he hurt her. As she walked home that day, she cleaned the memory of his attack from her mind. Only later to have the memories resurface when he did it again. His rage against Miriam would continue for four more years.

Once Miriam made it home that day, she did all she could to avoid her Mother and Father. She knew that her father liked to lovingly bounce her on his knee and chase her around the house, but her body couldn't stand anymore. When she walked up the walk way, Ruby was there waiting on her. Ruby ran up and gave her a big hug, almost knocking her down. The simple playful hug was unbearable for Miriam. She pushed Ruby back. This confused Ruby.

She began rambling, saying, "Miry, what's wrong did I hurt you. I'm sorry. Where have you been? You missed everything."

Ruby took Miriam by the hand and led her back down the walkway and continued to ramble about the events at the fair. "Do you know that Seth snuck and took a snoot and your daddy found out. He was so mad! I was laughing the whole time, because your daddy was chasing Seth around the whole fair."

Ruby noticed that Miriam wasn't laughing. Miriam loved it when her brothers got in trouble. Ruby stopped Miriam! "Miry are you okay? Why aren't you laughing?" asked Ruby.

Miriam didn't respond, she stood there staring at Ruby. She then handed her the necklace that the demon had given her. Ruby took the necklace and started jumping up and down. She gave Miriam another hug, and said, "Thanks Miry. It's so pretty. Where did you get it?"

There was still no response from Miriam. Her silence bothered Ruby, because Miriam talked all the time. Ruby took Miriam's silence as her not feeling well, since she did leave the fair early.

Ruby isn't the only person who would notice Miriam's new silence. Everyone, especially Naomi and Jeremiah began to notice that Miriam stopped talking. As time went on she became more and more of a recluse. Both her parents attempted to get Miriam to speak, but she didn't.

After a year of Miriam not speaking, everyone began to accept it. Naomi didn't like it, but she didn't know what to do about it. Her efforts were not successful.

David's Death ...

In the summer of 1954, Naomi's father David arrived home from an extensive time of working out of town. Bernice was there waiting for him, as usual. David's job with the railroad kept him out of town a lot. While he was away, Bernice's time was spent with Jessie, Gertrude, and their grandchildren. The grandchildren kept everyone busy.

Once David arrived, Gertrude said good-bye to Bernice. She knew that Bernice and David needed some alone time. At the end of the day, the two sat and talked for awhile. They reminisced on their life together. Once they had finished talking, they kissed, and said goodnight to each other.

Sometime in the middle of the night, David quietly passed away in his sleep, at the age of 70. His death was unexpected. Although he was advanced in age, that didn't stop him from working. His death heavily impacted Bernice, more than anyone. She accepted the fact that her husband perfect, but when she took her vows before God in 1903, she held them close to her heart.

David never revealed to Bernice of his infidelities. She never knew that he had conceived two children out of wedlock. After Mary Ann, Alecta, and Micah were killed, David drew away from Bernice and their children. Up until the day he died, he blamed himself for their deaths. Bernice noticed many years ago when David was distancing himself from their family, but she never questioned him about it, she just grew to accept his absence.

Chapter Thirteen

"Miry, you spoke," shouted Lydia.

Being home ...

BERNICE HELD DAVID'S BODY out long enough for Deborah and her family, Ruth, Lydia, and Jonathan to make it home. Their coming home was a great comfort to everyone. Their presence had been greatly missed.

After David was buried, everyone gathered at Bernice's house. Even though she had lost David, all of her family being there was soothing to her broken heart. All the family was there with the exception of Jessie and Miriam. Jessie made it well known throughout Bernice and David's marriage, which she didn't care for David, so she didn't attend the funeral. She did although prepared food for everyone to eat and had sent it to Bernice's house.

As soon as the funeral was over, Miriam ran to her great grandmother's house. For the past four years she had been spending most of her time with Jessie. Miriam no longer liked being around people and she was still refusing to speak. Being at Jessie's was ideal for her, because no one regularly visited Jessie and she didn't like talking.

Although Naomi hated the fact that her baby stopped spending time with the family, she allowed Miriam to spend a majority of her time with Jessie. She figured that even though Miriam wasn't speaking to them, that maybe she would eventually open up to Jessie.

While everyone was visiting with each other at Bernice's, Lydia excused herself to go and see Jessie and Miriam. Plus she hadn't spent any time with Miriam. Once she made it to Jessie's, she sat and talked with her for awhile. Jessie gave her a scarf and hat that she had knitted for her, Ruth, and Deborah.

"Here take these, and give the extra ones to Ruth and your Auntie Deb. I heard how cold it be in Chicago," said Jessie.

"Thanks Greatgran. Your right, it's really cold there. We will all put these to good use," said Lydia.

While talking with Jessie, Lydia noticed that Miriam was sitting off alone staring off into space. So she said, "Greatgran, what's wrong with Miry?"

"I don't know child. She's here every day sitting in the same spot, just looking off. She helps me around the house more than any child should. I know your Momma told you that she doesn't talk no more," said Jessie.

"Yes mam, she wrote us a few years ago and told us. We write her letters all the time, but Momma said after she reads them that she gives them back to her," said Lydia.

"Now, I told your Momma that this aint right. Something bad done happened to this child, but everybody think I'm crazy. I feel sorry for my baby. She can stay here as longs as she wants. We'll never know if anything happened to her, because she won't say anything," said Jessie.

"Umm, your right Greatgran, something had to have happened. You don't just all of a sudden stop talking in one day. I'm going to talk with her for awhile," said Lydia.

"Good luck," replied Jessie. Lydia went over and sat next to Miriam. She was now as big as Lydia. The last time Lydia saw her, Miriam was only nine. She was happy to be sitting next to her now, beautiful 16 year old sister. Lydia was still puzzled to why Miriam had stopped speaking.

Miriam turned and looked at Lydia when she sat down, but she didn't say a word. Lydia rested her hand on Miriam's knee, and said, "How have you been Miry?"

Miriam didn't speak. "Can you tell me why you think you're not speaking?" asked Lydia. Miriam didn't respond. Instead she started touching the necklace that Lydia was wearing. "Do you like it Miry?

My friend from Chicago gave it to me for my birthday. I think it's pretty too," said Lydia.

Lydia guided Miriam's head to face her directly. While holding onto Miriam's face, she said, "Miry please tell me why you don't speak. Did somebody hurt you? Please tell me what's wrong."

Lydia stared deeply into Miriam's eyes, praying that she could feel something to show her why Miriam was no longer speaking. She could see the pain in Miriam's eyes. She felt that something bad had happened to her.

Lydia then whispered to Miriam, "Come with me. We're going to go talk somewhere alone. Just me and you, nobody will know, okay."

Miriam then took Lydia by the hand and led her outside. They walked around to the side of the house and sat on a swing. They held hands and slowly rocked in the swing. Lydia began to speak, "You know Miry, sometimes things happen to people and they think that there's no way out. You know, all people act differently. Sometimes they act out or maybe, like you, they stop talking."

Lydia continued to talk. She looked over at Miriam to see that she was crying. Lydia got off the swing and kneeled down in front of Miriam. As Lydia looked up at Miriam, she could feel her pain. She then began crying. Miriam reached out and touched the tears coming from Lydia's face.

Lydia then squatted on her knees, placed her hands on top of Miriam's, and sobbing, she said, "Miry please talk to me. I know something is hurting you because I can feel your pain, it's ripping me up. I need Miry to come back to us."

Lydia rested her head on Miriam's lap and continued crying. Unexpectedly Miriam spoke, "Please don't cry Lydia." She then raised her head up! "Miry, you spoke," shouted Lydia. She then sat back beside Miriam on the swing and gave her a big hug, but Miriam wouldn't let go of her. The two hugged each other for a while before Miriam said, "Lydia, can you please take me to Chicago with you?"

Lydia pulled back from Miriam and looked at her. Lydia couldn't believe that Miriam wanted to leave New Hope. She knew that Miriam was a Daddy and Mommy's girl. Plus the last that Lydia was aware of, Miriam and Ruby were inseparable. "Chicago. You want to go to Chicago?" asked Lydia. Miriam didn't speak, but she nodded her head yes.

"Miry, you know that Momma and Daddy are not letting you go to Chicago. You're the baby girl. They'll have a fit! You see how they first acted when we left, then when Sarah left," said Lydia.

Miriam began pounding both her fists on the swing! Lydia had never seen Miriam this upset. She tried to calm her down. While still pounding the swing and now furiously turning her head from side to side, Miriam screamed, "I want to go with you!"

Lydia was dismayed over Miriam's reaction. She put her arms tightly around Miriam to prevent her from hurting herself. Once she had calmed her down, Lydia grabbed her by both wrists. Miriam's knuckles were covered in blood. Lydia was dumfounded.

Desperately trying to clean Miriam's hands, Lydia says, "Miry look at you! Your knuckles are all cut up now. You got to tell me what's going on. Come on, we need to talk to Momma and Daddy!"

Miriam snatched away from Lydia! "No!" she shouted. "You can't say anything. I promise, I kill myself if you do! Please, Lydia, I just want to go home with you."

Lydia sat looking at her sister in disbelief. She knew whatever was bothering her was serious. It hurt her to hear Miriam say that she would kill herself. "Okay Miry, calm down, if you don't want me to say anything to them, then fine. Miry you have to tell me what is so bad, what are you so afraid of, that you would even think about killing yourself if Momma or Daddy found out."

"I promise I will tell you, I promise. I just can't tell you anything until after we go to Chicago. Can you please wait," asked Miriam.

Unwillingly Lydia agreed. She knew that whatever was wrong with Miriam had to be something serious. Miriam making a promise was out of character. None of the Strong children had ever sworn or promised on anything for any reason. Those two things Jeremiah and Naomi absolutely forbade of them. Lydia had never heard the word promise come out of Miriam's mouth.

"Okay, okay! Calm down Miry. Let's see, you are 16 now. They let me leave when I was 16, so this may workout. I'll convince them to let you go. You know how important it is to them for us to all go to school. Now, you said you'll tell me what's wrong. As soon as we get to Chicago, you had better tell me," said Lydia.

Miriam's entire demeanor changed. She hugged Lydia as tight as she could, and said, "Thank you Lydia, thank you." Then in a almost unheard ton, as she was still hugging Lydia, she said, "Thank you God, it's finally over. He won't be able to hurt me anymore."

While the two were still hugging, Lydia clearly heard everything that Miriam said. She thought to herself, 'Jesus, who won't be able to hurt her anymore.'

They stood up, held hands, and went back inside to say good night to Jessie. Then the two girls headed to Bernice's house. Lydia had a very unsettling feeling about Miriam's statement, but she didn't want to upset her about it. She decided to wait until they went to Chicago to talk about it.

Everyone was still at Bernice's. All of the Strong children were there, even Sarah. She came down from Little Rock to attend the funeral. Once Lydia and Miriam entered the house, all of their siblings were sitting together, listening to Ruth and Sarah's stories about their new lives away from New Hope.

Everyone was shocked to see Miriam. After her talk with Lydia, she had a big smile on her face. She walked over to were her siblings were, and sat on Ruth's lap. She listened in on the stories being told. Busy talking, Ruth didn't pay attention to the fact that Miriam was almost as big as she was now. She was just happy to see her interacting with other people.

Old stories, new stories, and stories to be, filled the air. As Naomi and Jeremiah sat talking to Bernice and Wilton, Lydia walked up to them, spoke to everyone, and asked her parents if she could speak to them alone. Naomi and Jeremiah excused themselves and walked with Lydia outside.

Once outside, Lydia led the conversation, saying, "Momma, Daddy, I think that maybe Miriam should come back with us. Hold on! Before you say no, hear me out, please. She talked to me tonight at Greatgran's house. Something is bothering her, something has happened to her, but she can't talk about right now. I think it would be best for us to give her the time she needs to be able to tell us what's wrong. Pressuring her will only make it worse."

Lydia walked over and kneeled down next to her parents, and went on to say, "We all want what's best for Miry. She asked me; no I mean she begged me, if I would take her back with me. She told me that she would talk me to about whatever is going on with her, once we make it to Chicago. You both know that she'll be taken care of. She'll be around family. You both know how she likes school, so that won't be a problem," said Lydia.

Naomi and Jeremiah looked at each other. They knew the day would come when Miriam would want to go off like her sisters did. Jeremiah held his head down for a brief second, looked at Naomi, and said, "Well Naomi, we knew that it was coming."

He reached and held her hand, and said, "At least she spoke. I never thought she would do that again. She felt comfortable enough to talk to Lydia, maybe that's what she needs. I don't want my last daughter to leave, but look how good the other three are doing. What do you think?"

Naomi's eyes began filling with tears. She looked at Lydia, then back at Jeremiah, and said, "I know, I know, I know, but she's been so sad these past few years. I can't reach her, she won't talk to me. Since she finally talked, after four years of not saying a word, maybe being with her sisters is what she needs."

Naomi stood up and looked back towards the house, and said, "Did you see how happy my baby looked when yall walked in together. That's what I miss, the happy Miry! If leaving here and moving to Chicago is what it's going to take, then yes, she can go."

Jeremiah and Lydia stood up next to Naomi, and they all walked back inside. Ruth was inside passing out gifts that they had brought to the family from Chicago. Jokingly Lydia said, "Hey Ruthie Strong, didn't I tell you we were giving the presents out together."

With a laugh, Ruth responded, "Yes you did little Jessie, but you were taking too long. Besides, big head Seth and James was acting like kids, so I had to give the babies their presents." Both Seth and James dived onto Ruth and started tickling her and Miriam.

"All right, all right, you Strongs had better settle down," said Jeremiah.

Miriam got down off Ruth's lap, and sat on the floor next to her. "Okay Poppa Strong and Momma Strong, come sit down, we got something special for yall," said Ruth.

Naomi was stunned. Her children all being there together was gift enough for her. She and Jeremiah sat down next to Ruth and Lydia. Naomi's gift was first. Ruth handed her a burgundy, velvet covered box. Before she could open the box, Naomi's face was gleaming. She then opened the box, gave Jeremiah the lid, and pulled back the wrappings covering the gift. She sat the box down on her lap, and covered her mouth with her hands.

"Naomi, are you alright?" asked Jeremiah.

"Oh my goodness, girls," said Naomi.

Everyone waited for Naomi to reveal her gift. From the box, she pulled out two wooden picture frames. She placed both of them up to her chest, looked at Jeremiah, and smiled. "Jeremiah look at this," she said.

Jeremiah took the picture frames from Naomi and looked at them. One was Ruth's degree from college, the other one was Lydia's degree. Jeremiah was flabbergasted! Both he and Naomi gratefully hugged Ruth and Lydia. Everyone in the room was overjoyed that not one, but two members of their small family actually had a college degree. The entire atmosphere in the room was filled with joy.

In the midst of all the excitement, Lydia handed Jeremiah a leather case, the size of a book. He graciously received the case. "Ooh, thank you baby, the case feels so smooth. I believe its leather. Thank you girls," said Jeremiah. Lydia laughed and said, "Daddy, you have to open it."

Jeremiah unzipped the case. Inside was a holy bible. In the bottom right hand corner, the words, THE STRONGS, had been stitched on. Jeremiah ran his fingers across the words, THE STRONGS. He didn't think he could get any happier. He was speechless.

"Daddy, do you like it?" asked Ruth. He nodded his head yes, and just sat there and stared at his new bible.

"Daddy we know that you have Grandma Ruth's bible, but it's falling apart. So we decided to get you a new one. That's what the case is for, to put Grandma Ruth's bible in. Now you can carry your new bible to church," said Ruth.

Jeremiah, so touched by the gift, didn't know how to respond. Eventually, he said, "This is the most thoughtful thing I've ever seen."

Ruth and Lydia were so happy about the receptions they received from their gifts. They still had two more gifts to hand out. Ruth reached down and handed Miriam a box, wrapped lavender paper. She carefully removed the paper and opened the box. Inside were a brush, comb, and mirror. Each piece had been hand painted with lavender colored flowers, with the letters, M, S, carved on. Both Ruth and Lydia knew that purple was Miriam's favorite color.

Just like their mother, Bernice, and Jessie, the four Strong girls had very long, thick, and cold black hair. Each of the women in the family took great pride in how beautiful their hair was. When the Strong girls were smaller, Naomi would sit and brush their hair for awhile. This was her bonding time with her daughters. Miriam loved her gift.

The last gift they had to give was to Wilton. Lydia walked over and handed him his gift. Then she said, "Here you go Wilton. I know we haven't met you, but Momma has told us so many good things about you in her letters to us. You're family, so we didn't want to leave you out. We hope you like it."

Wilton was surprised, he didn't expect a gift. He was content with just being in the company of everyone. He then opened his box. Inside where carving tools. These would really come in handy when he did his wood work. He was overjoyed, and said, "Thank you girls, this is so nice of you." Ruth and Lydia both gave Wilton a hug.

After the last gift was given out, everyone began to leave. Ruth stood up and said, "Hey, I have an idea! How about all the girls, you to Momma and Aunt Deb, spend the night here with Granny."

"Ruth, that's a fine idea. I don't really want to be alone," said Bernice. All the women in the family were all on board with this idea. All the men in the family left. After the women finished leaning up, and dressing down for bed, Bernice walked up to where they all sat. She was holding a plate of cookies, and said, "Look girls what I have. I managed to keep these from Jonathan."

They all laughed and started eating their cookies, while catching up on lost time. Miriam laid on Naomi's lap as Naomi brushed her hair with her new brush that Lydia and Ruth had given her. Naomi sat back and observed how happy her girls were. She knew that the last of her daughters was about to leave, but she accepted it. She wanted the same thing for Miriam that her other daughters had, happiness.

Over at Jeremiah's house were his sons Seth and James, Andrew with the twins Thomas Lee and Calvin, Jonathan, William and his sons Don Jr., William Jr., and Norman. Wilton was also there, but he didn't spend the night. Bernice's brother Floyd didn't come down for the funeral. The men sat around most of the night talking, but when everyone began getting tired, Jeremiah excused himself. All the others camped out in the front room.

Jeremiah took Ruth's bible and placed it in his new leather case. It fit perfectly. He was so thankful to the girls for being so thoughtful.

He flipped through the pages of his new bible. He noticed on the first page of the bible, that Lydia and Ruth had made him a family tree. He didn't think his gift from the girls could have gotten any better. Gratitude filled Jeremiah's heart.

He then did what he did every night, talked and prayed to God. He got down on his knees, bowed his head, and said, "My heavenly Father, blessed is your name. Lord, I am so thankful to you for my many blessings. Lord, I thank you for hearing my prayers. I don't know how many times to thank you, so I'll continue to do it every day. Lord your praises will continually come from my mouth. Lord, I also thank you for my wife, all my children, and my cousin Wilton being here with us. Thank you for showing mercy on us all. Lord, I pray that you will continue to bless and keep us in all our ways. In your son Jesus' name I pray for these things, Amen."

Chapter Fourteen

She took the knife, pulled it out in front of her and with all the strength in her body, she fatally plunged the knife into her abdomen!

Both Lydia and Miriam Are Gone ...

THE MORNING AFTER DAVID'S funeral, the sun shined bright on New Hope. Jeremiah walked outside with a cup of coffee and stared out at the beautifulness of the things that God had made. Dew barely saturated the head of the grass, while the chirping of the birds filled the air. The flowers were bright and at their full bloom.

But as Jeremiah looked a bit closer at the flowers near his house, he noticed two dead flowers. It was only two, and they looked out of place to Jeremiah. He picked the flowers and held them in his hand.

Over at Bernice's, everyone was being woke up by the smell of dry salt meat, homemade biscuits, and fresh black coffee. As everyone was clearing the sleep from their eyes, Bernice noticed that Lydia wasn't there. She figured she must have walked over to Jessie's house to check on her.

Bernice proceeded to fix everyone else a plate. They all sat around, talked, and enjoyed their breakfast. They were all trying to enjoy each other as much as they could, because Deborah and all who came from out of town, were leaving in a couple of days. As they sat eating breakfast the door opened. It was Jessie, walking in on her cane. "Morning yall," said Jessie.

Everyone said hello and they all gave Jessie a hug, and helped her to her seat. "Momma is Lydia at your house?" asked Bernice.

"No baby, she came over last night and got Miry. That's the last I seen of her. Why?" asked Jessie.

"Oh, I was just wondering. She wasn't here when we woke up this morning," said Bernice.

"Umm, I just noticed that. Maybe she went to the house. Ruth, take Sarah and go see for me," said Naomi. Ruth and Sarah headed off to the house to see if Lydia was there.

"This is what I love to see, all my beautiful girls in one room. It makes my 80 something year old heart feel good. I bet yall stayed up half the night talking," said Jessie.

"Yes Granny. Your daughter wouldn't let us go to sleep. She was trying to fatten us up with homemade cookies," said Naomi.

Bernice laughed, and said, "Ahh Naomi, I didn't do such a thing."

"I'm just glad yall are enjoying each other. It's good to see everybody so happy. This is what it's all about," said Jessie. They all continued talking and enjoying their time together.

Over at the Strong's house, Ruth and Sarah had arrived. Jeremiah, Andrew, William, and Jonathan were standing outside. Ruth and Sarah gave everyone a hug. "What are you girls doing out so early?" asked Andrew.

"Momma sent us to get Lydia. Granny fixed all of us breakfast and they want Lydia to come and eat," said Sarah. Jeremiah smiled, and said, "Now you know Lydia is not here. Maybe she's at your Greatgran's."

"No Daddy, Greatgran is at Granny's house with Momma them," said Sarah.

Jeremiah quickly thought to himself, 'Where could she be. Maybe she's with a friend of hers.' He then asked, "Do she have any friends she would've gone to see?"

"Daddy no, we don't have any friends left here, everyone done moved away," said Sarah. Then panic set in for everyone. It was true, all the children that grew up with the Strong children had moved away. So Jeremiah rounded everyone up at his house. He sent everyone off in pairs to search for Lydia. He, Ruth, and Sarah went back to Bernice's house.

Once they made it to Bernice's, Jeremiah asked, "Has Lydia come back here?" All the women looked at each other confused. "What do you mean? She's should have been at the house," said Naomi.

Now really worried, Jeremiah sat down next to Jessie. He looked up at everyone and said, "No, she's not at the house and she hasn't been there!"

Jessie placed her hand on his knee, and said, "Calm down, let's all just calm down and think. Now, Bernice when is the last that you saw of her?"

Bernice became concerned. She sat down and started thinking. Then she said, "We all went to sleep last night in this house. She was here with us. Before daylight, I walked around to make sure everyone was covered up, and she was here. But when I got up to cook breakfast at daylight, she wasn't."

This was unusual for no one to know where Lydia was, this was a very small community. Everyone, including Jessie, began to panic. Jeremiah walked over and held Naomi, who was now crying. "Jeremiah, we have to go look for her! Come on yall!" said Naomi.

Everyone readied themselves to go search for her. "Wait! Everybody that was at the house with me is out looking. Naomi sits here with Granny. I'll take Ruth and Sarah with me, and we'll go help them look. Please baby, just calm down, and don't worry, we'll find her." said Jeremiah. Naomi did as Jeremiah said. She and the other women began to pray.

The men hadn't found any sign of Lydia. William had gotten Wilton, Ronnie, Kent, Harold, and some more people to help them search for Lydia.

Morning had turned into night; still there was no sign of Lydia. Jeremiah was so desperate that he went to his boss, Bill for help. Once he made it to Bill's house, he told him about Lydia being missing. He also told him that they had been looking for her every since morning. Bill didn't question Jeremiah; he swiftly gathered a group of local white men to help in the search.

The whites and blacks lived in separate quarters. Bill ordered them to put color aside and help look for Lydia. Some of the whites refused unless he paid them to help. He didn't waste any time arguing, he paid them all for helping. The blacks were on their side of town and the whites on their side, carefully looked for Lydia for two days. There was still no sign of her.

With all that was going on surrounding Lydia's disappearance, the family from Chicago hadn't realized it was time for them to return, for work and school. Deborah went to talk to Naomi and Jeremiah; she saw how heartbroken they both were. She hesitated to speak, then she said, "Naomi, Jeremiah, I hate to leave like this, but we have to go back to work. We're going to be leaving out tomorrow."

Naomi reached over and held onto Deborah. As she was crying, she said, "I know yall have jobs to get back to. We have more than enough people helping us. Go home; we'll let you know something as soon as we find out something."

The two sisters continued to hold and comfort each other. Nearly every person searching was at the Strong house, inside and outside. This was the first time that a female, black or white had gone missing here. Jeremiah and Naomi, along with all the others, couldn't think of any place that Lydia would be, without letting anyone know where she was.

Miriam was taking Lydia's disappearance especially hard. She felt somewhat alone again. After talking to her sister a couple of days ago about going back to Chicago with her, it now seemed, that was not happening. She now worried that she would never see her sister again. All the noise and commotion of the people became too much for her. She ran off into the dark. Little did she know, the man who had been raping her for the past four years, (the demon as she called him) sneakily followed her.

Miriam's demon caught up with her and dragged her to his house. She thought that her nightmare and pain of being raped by him was over. Ever since her family had been down from Chicago, she had been able to avoid him.

He was angry with Miriam. He then began with his sick routine style of raping her, while continuing to instill fear. He had controlled her mind for the past four years. He now knew that she was planning to go back to Chicago. As he lay on top of her, raping her, he spoke in her ear, saying, "I know that you plan on going to Chicago, but I'm telling you that you're not! You are not leaving me, you understand!"

He continued to violently rape her, while continuing to fill her mind with fear. Miriam was in extreme pain. The force of his rape was damaging her body. He was rapping her so hard, unknown to either of them, that she started hemorrhaging inside. Her pain seemed to only fuel his rage. As he continued raping her, over and over, for over an hour, he then said, "If you want your sister Lydia back, you'll get Chicago out your mind!"

This terrified her. Her instinct told her that he had done something to Lydia, something worse than what he had been doing to her. As he continued to rape Miriam, crying she asked, "Where is she?"

He then stopped! He climbed from on top of her. While grinning and pulling up his pants, he said, "Oh you don't worry yourself any about that. All you need to know is, if you think about leaving again, maybe one of your other pretty sisters will disappear. You just tell your folks that you done changed your mind about Chicago. If you do that, you'll save your family the pain of another daughter disappearing." He stood over Miriam taking pride in her pain.

Miriam lay on the floor in pain. Now she was blaming herself for Lydia's disappearance. She thought, 'If I leave New Hope, it's no telling what he'll do. This is my entire fault.' Miriam was already scared, now she felt anger and guilt.

"Did you hear me black girl?" he asked.

"Yes, I heard you. Please don't hurt anybody else, I promise, I won't go to Chicago," responded Miriam.

"Good, now get up and get out of here!" he said.

He then left out of the room. Miriam began to put her clothes on to leave. As she got ready to walk out the door, she felt something under her foot. She reached down to pick it up. It was Lydia's necklace! Miriam began to cry, and softly said, "This is Lydia's, she was here. Oh God he killed her! This is my fault!"

Miriam was so nervous that in the process of escaping, she dropped the necklace on the floor.

Before he could say anything to her, she had fled out the front door. He didn't go after her; he figured she would do as she was told.

Miriam didn't go home, instead she went to Jessie's, and she knew that no one was there. She now many emotions going on inside her mind as well as her heart. She felt great sorrow and guilt over Lydia. She figured if she told her mother and father, that they would be mad at her. She actually blamed herself for Lydia's disappearance. It became too much for her young damaged mind to tolerate, she had a nervous breakdown.

Miriam sat on the floor rocking back and forth while clutching her knees. Then, she rocked faster and faster! She started rambling. As she cried uncontrollably, she said, "This is my fault, this is my fault! My fault, my fault, my fault! No, no, no, I don't want the demon to hurt her! Hurt me, hurt me, I'm sorry Lydia, I'm so sorry Momma," she rambled on and on.

Miriam, with her entire body shaking and trembling profusely, jumped up off the floor and ran into the kitchen! She grabbed one of Jessie's knifes, and sat on the floor. With the knife in her hand, Miriam suddenly began screaming!

"THIS IS THE ONLY WAY, HE WON'T STOP; HE JUST WON'T STOP! God tell Momma, tell Daddy I'm so sorry. I won't cause nobody anymore hurt. I'm sorry, I'm sorry," … she rambled. As Miriam continued to scream aloud, she took the knife, pulled it out in front of her and with all the strength in her body, she fatally plunged the knife into her abdomen!

Miriam took her own life thinking she was the blame for Lydia's disappearance. Along with imagining that she would have to stay in Arkansas and continue being raped, became too much for her. She died a sad and lost child. Being raised with the word of God instilled in you every day, isn't enough to protect you from the wages of sin if you don't comprehend and obey God's words.

Miriam's demon, by force, was able to undo the years of God's words that her parents had instilled in her. The demon, a.k.a rapist, sought out to destroy innocence. He found what he was looking for, in a child. Because she was immature, naive, and trusting he was able to gradually undo everything that she had been taught. He replaced all that she knew, with fear. Just like the devil, Miriam's rapist came to steal, kill, and destroy. He was able to do all three.

First he stole the innocence and purity of his prey. Secondly, his actions directly led to Miriam taking her own life. Thirdly, he destroyed a town, a community; a community already facing the trials of hatred and racism. He was able to cunningly deceive his neighbors.

Lydia and Miriam were not his only victims, there were many before and after. He destroyed much more than their communities; he also destroyed his own salvation. One thing their murderer was not looking for was righteousness.

He had the opportunity, as we all do to choose right or to choose wrong. He made his choice at a young age to cause destruction, with the assumption that he would be able to accept whatever punishment was due to him on his judgment day. One thing he never counted on was his crimes committed in darkness, eventually coming to light.

Chapter Fifteen

Why would this child take her own life?

Miriam is Found ...

Bᴀᴄᴋ ᴀᴛ ᴛʜᴇ Sᴛʀᴏɴɢ's house, the people helping with the search had thinned out. All of the family was still there. Lydia's disappearance had impacted everyone in the community. The news of her disappearance spread fast.

As the family sat together praying, there was knock on the door. It was about 10 or so black men at the door. No one there had seen them before. William walked over and introduced his self and the family. One of the men shook William's hand, and said, "How yall? I'm Napoleon Martin. Much obliged to you all. Me, also these here boys are from Goosehollow and them there parts. We got word that one of your youngins went missing."

"Yes sir, come on in, my 22 year old niece. Do yall know something that might be of help?" asked William.

"No, we don't know anything about it, but we did have something we needed to tell her folks," said Napoleon. Just then Jeremiah walked over to the men. He shook Napoleon's hand, and said, "I'm her daddy. You can talk to me."

Jeremiah told the men to have a seat, were they could find one. He and Napoleon sat down to talk. Napoleon led the conversation, as everyone intensely listened, saying, "I live in a small town, such as this one. Some of the men with me live there or close by. In 1949 one of our daughters went missing. After that, young girls were coming up missing every year, up to now. Two weeks ago, a 10 year old child went missing. She had been outside playing with the other youngins, but they all went home. When she didn't show up after dark, her folks went looking for her. All they found was one of her white shoes that she had been wearing. All together it's been four. We haven't found a hide or hair of none of them. So when we got word that a youngin from here went missing, we wanted to come and help. Maybe if we all work together we can put an end to this."

Jeremiah, along with everyone else, was alarmed. They hadn't heard of anyone else to have disappeared. Lydia's disappearance, now seemed like it could be more than a simple disappearance.

"So you say the first girl was in '49," said Jeremiah.

"Yeah, '49. Her folks woke up one morning and she was gone. All of the other ones went missing at night to," said Napoleon.

"Umm, the same thing happened with my Lydia. Her and the women folk all stayed together that night, and the next morning she was just gone," said Jeremiah.

"These youngins aint just missing, something done happened to them. Something bad, that's keeping them from being able to come home. Whoever is doing this is doing it at night," said Napoleon.

Although Jeremiah and everyone else didn't want to believe that they would have to possibly face the fact that Lydia was not coming home.

As everyone continued to talk, Jessie got the urge for a fresh pinch of snuff. She asked Jonathan to walk with her to the house so she could get a pinch. She told everyone that she would be back shortly.

As the two walked to Jessie's house, Jonathan trying to lightened Jessie's spirit, says, "Granny, I know where you hide your snuff. We all do."

It did lighten her spirit a little. She laughed a little and they continued walking. Once they arrived, Jonathan helped Jessie inside. When she first entered the house, she saw Miriam on the floor. She didn't think anything of it at first glance. She yelled out, "Miry, get yourself off that floor!"

Instincts told her that something was wrong. So she walked over to Miriam. In disbelief, she saw that Miriam was hurt. Initially she didn't know how bad. She then noticed that Miriam was covered in blood. She slung her cane from her hand! She fell to the floor! She slowly turned Miriam over. Her hand was still clutched to the knife inside of her.

Jessie felt the life leave her body. She started screaming, picked Miriam up, and held her in her arms. By now Jonathan was sitting on the floor next to her. He was also in disarray. Sitting on the floor, holding Miriam, Jessie desperately yelled, "Go, go, and get some help!" Jonathan didn't think twice, he ran out the door to get help.

Jessie remained there holding Miriam's cold lifeless body. She had been laying there on the floor dead for over two hours. As Jessie rocked back and forth, she screamed and cried. "God please, please take me! Bring her back! Just please bring her back! Miry! Why did you hurt yourself? Dear Lord, if you hear me, please help her!" shouted Jessie.

Jonathan had arrived at the Strong's house. He had run so hard that he had fallen several times. In a panic, he burst into the door! He startled everyone.

"Jonathan, what's wrong?" shouted Jeremiah.

Jonathan was visibly shaken. He couldn't get his words out. He fell onto Jeremiah's shoulder, attempting to catch his breath. By now everyone was frightened; they didn't know what to take from Jonathan's behavior. Jeremiah was finally able to calm him down. Everyone dreadfully waited to hear what he had to say.

Naomi couldn't take it. She feared what he was trying to say, so she covered her ears and closed her eyes tightly. Jonathan then blurted out, "It's Miry, it's Miry! She stabbed herself in the stomach. Blood, knife, dead," ... he continued to ramble.

Jeremiah and the others didn't ask any questions, they immediately dashed off to Jessie's house. Even with her ears covered Naomi still was able to hear what Jonathan said. She couldn't believe it; he must be mistaking she thought. Behind the others, she charged out the door! The entire way to Jessie's, she prayed and begged God for it not to be.

Once Jeremiah arrived at Jessie's, he burst through the door! All he initially saw was Jessie sitting on the floor holding Miriam. As he got closer, his fears were becoming true. He fell to the floor and took Miriam's body out of Jessie's grip.

He screamed! In Jeremiah's mind Miriam's lifeless body triggered a memory he had buried deep. As he sat on the floor rocking back and forth, crying, he begged God, "Lord! Why, why, why my baby? I've did all you've asked of me! I want my baby back!"

Everyone in the room was confused and distraught over the loss of Miriam. They were all thinking the same thing, 'Why would this child take her own life.'

By now Naomi entered the front door. Her body was drained of all its strength from dealing with one child missing, to another being possibly dead. Her doubts quickly became reality when she saw Jeremiah holding Miriam. She no longer could walk, so she attempted to crawl. Once she gotten close enough to Jeremiah and Miriam, she saw the blood covering the floor. Seeing the blood caused Naomi to pass out. Once she fainted, Norman and Calvin carried her in to lay her on Jessie's bed. Ruth and Sarah then went into the room to stay with their mother.

As Naomi lay there unconscious, a vision entered her mind. Naomi's perception of the vision was that it was reality. There was brightness, an almost serene light. She looked down at herself and wondered what was happening. She then began to walk toward the light. As she got closer, figures started forming into people. Her steps got faster! Once she made it to the figures, she saw that they were Lydia and Miriam.

The girls were sitting in a field of green grass surrounded by large yellow sunflowers. Lydia was sitting in a chair with Miriam sitting on the ground in front of her. Lydia was brushing Miriam's hair. The two girls were laughing and talking to one another. Naomi stood directly in front of them and then grabbed her mouth in amazement. "Lydia, Miry, it's really you," she said.

Naomi fell on Miriam's legs as she sat on the ground. She began to cry. Miriam began rubbing Naomi's head, while attempting to console her. "Momma, why are you crying," she asked.

Naomi responded, "I'm crying because you're not at home." She raised herself up and kneeled beside her daughters. Lydia continued to brush Miriam's hair. Naomi couldn't understand their nonchalant attitude. Miriam reached out and touched Naomi's face, and said, "I'm not at home, but look, I'm with Lydia."

Naomi placed her hand over Miriam's hand and said, "I'm glad to see that you're with Lydia, but I don't understand why either of you had to leave."

Lydia gently pushed Miriam to get her to rise to her feet, they both stood up. Lydia then reached down and grabbed Naomi by the hand. All three stood together holding hands. Naomi crying, while Lydia and Miriam smiled with contentment.

"Momma, I didn't ask to leave nor did I know that I was leaving, but I'm gone. What had to be done has been done. I can only accept my circumstances. I left before Miry. I didn't know she was coming, but she did. We're here now. Look around at how beautiful this place is, how peaceful it is here. We no longer have to be afraid of anything or anyone," said Lydia.

"Please tell me who or what were you afraid of? That's what I was there for, to comfort and protect you," said Naomi.

"Look Momma, you did everything that you were supposed to do. You couldn't help me because I was taken in the middle of the night. You couldn't help Miry because she didn't know how to ask you for help. Everything that you and Daddy had taught her was being replaced by fear of someone more mentally mature."

"Momma, do not cry for us, because we are in a better place, a wonderful place. We are not worried that someone will hurt us or that we will have pain, because those things don't exist here," said Miriam.

"If you ever loved us then you'll let us go and you will stop crying out of sorrow and start crying out of joy! For, you to one day will be in this place. You will see it for all its beauty, you will also be free," said Lydia.

Naomi stood intensely listening to every word that her daughters spoke, for she didn't know if she would ever hear their voice again. Her tears were slowly drying as she began to comprehend what her daughters were saying.

Lydia loosened her hands and stood directly in front of Naomi. She then held Naomi by both sides of her face and said, "Momma, I love you so much. In my life on earth, you were above all. You and Daddy did well by all of your children, you can be thankful for that. You don't have anything to feel guilty about. This was the time God saw it fit for us to be with him. We will be here waiting on the day until it's time for all of you to join us."

Lydia then took a couple of steps back, Miriam stood in front of Naomi. She then took Naomi by both of her hands, and said, "Momma, I love you very much. It's not your fault or Daddy's that you couldn't get through to me. You both tried, but my wounds were too deep and

I was told not to tell anyone about my pain. Those wounds have been healed and the pain is no more. Please be strong for us and everyone at home that needs you."

Miriam reached over and took Lydia's hand, while Lydia held Naomi's hand. Naomi tightly held both of her daughters hand as if it was the last time. Her tears had now completely dried. She couldn't explain what she was witnessing, but she didn't question it. Her daughter were happy and safe, but most importantly, they were together. Seeing them like this was very pleasing to Naomi.

"Momma tell everyone at home to stop looking for my body, because they won't find it. The trespasser who is responsible for hurting us will be seen for what he is. All that he done to us in darkness will come to light, when God says that it is time. Save everyone a lot of time and heartache and stop looking," said Lydia.

"You have to go back now Momma. Everyone at home needs you. Let Daddy know that we're okay. Oh, and tell him that Grandpa Seth and Grandma Ruth are so very proud of him. She also wanted him to know that her necklace was taken by the person that killed her," said Miriam.

Naomi noticeably didn't understand what Miriam meant by her last comment. Both Lydia and Miriam turned around to look behind them. Standing 12 feet or so, were Jeremiah's parents, Seth and Ruth. They both waved and blew a kiss towards Naomi. She became overwhelmed and returned their affection.

Lydia and Miriam kissed Naomi for the last time and walked off towards their grandparents. Naomi stood and watched her daughters join Ruth and Seth.

As all four faded off into the field of sunflowers, Naomi heard someone calling her name. She turned around to see who it was, but no one was there. She continued to hear her named being called. She closed her eyes and laid down in the field where she stood. With her name echoing in her hearing, she opened her eyes. She saw that she was no longer in the field, but instead at home in her bed. As she cleared her eyes, she began to see Jeremiah standing over her. She pulled him down to her and hugged him.

Still deeply heartbroken, Jeremiah asked, "Are you okay? You passed out and everyone was worried."

"I am now," she replied.

Jeremiah sat down on the bed next to her. He started softly caressing her face. "I'm glad to hear that. I've lost enough today, I won't be able to stand it if I lost you. I was so worried that you wouldn't wake up," he said.

"I'm sorry to have worried you so. I'm okay, so please don't waste any unnecessary stress over me. Now, where is everyone," asked Naomi.

"Well just about everybody is still here. Our house has the most room, so Momma and Granny are here. I didn't want them to be left alone. I hate to bring this up, but they took Miriam's body to the church for the funeral tomorrow. We still haven't found a sign of Lydia anywhere. I don't won't you to worry, I'll take care of the funeral and the search for Lydia," said Jeremiah.

Talking about his daughters in this unfortunate manner, caused Jeremiah to cry. Naomi rose up and held him. She warmly and affectionately comforted him, and said, "Lydia and Miry are okay."

Jeremiah, thinking the grieve had took over her train of thought, responded, "What do you mean?"

"Please don't think I'm crazy, because I'm not. I saw both of my babies. They were safe and happy, because they were with God. I didn't see God, but I'm telling you that I saw them. Believe what I'm telling you Jeremiah. We are going to bury our daughter's body tomorrow, and we're going to stop looking for our other daughter's body. You know that I've never lied to you or ever will. I need you to trust me on this. We're going to be okay," said Naomi.

At the time Jeremiah was so distraught that he didn't know what to believe. He kissed Naomi and said, "You know I trust you, that's not the problem. I just have to try to handle this my own way right now."

"Okay Jeremiah," said Naomi.

Jeremiah kissed Naomi again and told her he was going outside for a while. As he walked out to the smoke house, he remembered the two dead flowers that he had found in his yard. Out of anger and frustration, he threw the flowers on the ground, and said, "Two dead flowers for my two dead daughter."

He continued walking towards the smoke house to try to gather his thoughts. Once he entered the smoke house, he lit his lantern, and kneeled to pray.

"Lord, Lord, Lord, I don't have an idea on what to think or how to think right now. I'm mad, but I know that's not going to help anything.

I just don't get it. Why me Lord, why my girls? Why was I not taken away, instead of them. If I ever needed you, it's right now. I'm feeling real low God. I thought I did everything that I was supposed to do by you. Now I feel like my whole world is falling down. If I still deserve it, Lord God, please show me mercy," said Jeremiah.

Jeremiah kept his head down and began to sob. His pain was now interfering with his faith; this did not please him. He felt as if his spirit had been broken. As he kneeled there with his head down, he heard a voice, saying, 'Jeremiah I am here, I've always been with you. I hear your pleas and I see your sorrow. I never once told you that there would be no pain. I prepared you to deal with your pain. Now is the time for you to use what you have in your understanding concerning faith and strength in me. Not once did I put more on you than I knew that you would be able to bear. Go past your sadness and sorrow, and see what I see. It's there, but only you can find it and put it to use. Now, stand up!'

Jeremiah obediently stood to his feet. After hearing the voice, he instantly felt a sense of relief. He also now felt guilty for ever letting his faith lack. He then begged the Lord for forgiveness. Before he entered the smoke house he felt sorrow for himself and his circumstances. He had doubt about whether God would carry him through his storm. He made up his mind before leaving the smoke house to never again doubt the Lord.

Chapter Sixteen

Jeremiah, what's wrong? It looks like you saw a ghost

The Funeral ...

THE DAY HAD ARRIVED for Miriam's body to be laid to rest. The small church was packed. Black people from adjoining towns also attended the funeral. The Strong family sat at the front of the church. A neighboring pastor performed the funeral ceremony. Many people, including Ruby, got up a spoke of memories of Miriam's life.

The Strong family received so much support from their neighbors. Both Jeremiah and Naomi held themselves together remarkably considering their loss. Before everyone left the church, Jeremiah thanked everyone for showing up and offering comfort to him and his family.

After the services were over, Ruby (Miriam's best friend) approached Jeremiah and Naomi. She gave them both a hug and offered her sympathy. She then said, "Mr. Strong, Mrs. Strong, there's something I want to give you. The day that Miry stopped talking, she gave me this beautiful necklace. I think she would want you to have it. She didn't tell me where she got it from though, but here it is."

Ruby reached inside her purse and pulled out the necklace that Miriam had given her. As she was handing the necklace to Naomi, Jeremiah took it out of her hand. With a puzzling look on his face, he thanked Ruby.

"Jeremiah, what's wrong? It looks like you saw a ghost," said Naomi. She quickly began to wonder why he looked confused.

Jeremiah stood there with his heart racing, hoping that this familiar looking necklace didn't belong to his mother. He knew that in one of the stones on Ruth's necklace, his father had carved the letters, R and S. He closely inspected the stones. After carefully inspecting the necklace, to his horror, he saw the letters, R and S carved in one of the stones. He grabbed Naomi by the hand and ran home. Once they arrived at their house, he sat Naomi down to talk to her about the necklace. Naomi attentively sat wondering what was going on.

Jeremiah calmly stated, "This is my momma's necklace. What I didn't tell you or anybody else, is that when I saw my momma's dead body, she wasn't wearing her necklace. Everybody knew Momma never took this necklace off. Look, right here, R and S! Daddy carved this letters on this stone for her."

At this very second, Naomi began recalling something that Miriam had told her in her vision. She anxiously stood to her feet and began pacing. Looking at Jeremiah, she said, "I need to tell you something and I really need you to believe me."

Jeremiah reassured Naomi that he would believe whatever she had to tell him. She continued and said, "Remember last night when I told you that I saw Lydia and Miry?"

"Yeah, I remember," replied Jeremiah.

"Well, Miry told me something that your momma said. At the time I didn't know what she meant, but now it's beginning to make more sense," said Naomi.

"Okay, so what did she tell you?" asked Jeremiah.

"She told me that your momma told her to tell you that whoever taken from her by the person who killed her," said Naomi.

Jeremiah stood to his feet in amazement, and said, "Are you serious? Are you sure that's what she said?"

"I'm positive that's what she said. I didn't understand what she meant because I didn't know anything about a necklace. I saw them both," said Naomi.

"You saw who," asked Jeremiah.

"Your momma and daddy. They were standing off behind Lydia and Miry. They said that they were proud of you. Before I woke up, they both waved and blew a kiss my way," said Naomi.

Hearing this was hard to believe to Jeremiah, but not unbelievable. He sat and soaked in what Naomi had just told him. She then asked him if he was okay and did he believe her.

He replied, "I'm okay, what you told me just caught me off guard. You know that I believe you, I always will. How did they look, where they okay?"

"Yes they were okay. They both looked very well. Your daddy was a lot taller than your momma. He was holding his hat in his hand and holding your momma. He had a grey patch of hair at the front of his hairline. Your momma was wearing a beautiful purple dress. Jeremiah she is so beautiful, she had her hair pulled up in a bun," said Naomi.

Jeremiah's emotions took over him, and he began to cry with joy in his heart. "Naomi, this is hard to believe, but I know that it is true. How could you explain things about my folks that I never told you. Daddy did have a grey patch of hair at the front of his head and Momma was buried in a purple dress. I believe she was trying to lead me to whoever killed her by this necklace," said Jeremiah.

"Okay, we need to sit down and start figuring things out. How did your momma's necklace get from Kentucky all the way to New Hope? Once the necklace made it to New Hope, who then gave it to Miry?" asked Naomi.

Jeremiah desperately tried to put two and two together. "Well I know that I didn't bring it here. I know that Harold, Ronnie, or Kent didn't bring it here. Neither one of them was ever around Miry that we knew of. So, who else could it be?" he asked.

Naomi was also trying to figure this out, and said, "I hate to say this, so please don't get mad, but what about Wilton. Miry was always at his house, her and Ruby. Most of the times she went to his house without Ruby."

"You know what Naomi, I don't know why, but that makes so much sense. It would explain so much. But if Wilton had the necklace, that means he killed Momma," said Jeremiah.

"This would explain a lot Jeremiah. Momma Ruth said that whoever had her necklace is the same person who killed her. Why would Wilton do something so awful to his own auntie," asked Naomi.

Jeremiah began to get angry. He then said, "I don't know why or if he did it, but I'm sure as hell going to find out! Come on, let's go find him."

115

By the time that Jeremiah and Naomi had made it back to the church, Miriam's body had been buried. The crowd was beginning to thin out. All the people that remained, attempted to console Jeremiah and Naomi. Both of them frantically looked through the crowd hoping to see Wilton. They asked around, but no one had seen him.

Jeremiah was angry, but he didn't want to jump to conclusions or assume that Wilton was guilty until he had spoken to him face to face. His daughter having his mother's necklace in her possession was confusing to him.

After the church grounds were cleared of all the people, Jeremiah and Naomi still hadn't found Wilton. Both of them decided to go to his house. Once they entered his house, they called out for him, but he didn't answer.

Naomi walked over to the window to pull down the fabric that was covering the window. Once the sunlight shinned through the window, they were stunned. The house was in complete disarray. It appeared that no human being lived there.

Naomi went into the next room. She saw what looked like a place that Wilton slept. She had to cover her nose because the smell in the room was strongly invasive. She carefully pulled back the top layer of covering. The pad underneath was covered with blood. The blood wasn't moist, it had dried. The amount of blood on the pad was shocking Naomi.

She turned to run out of the room. As she started to run out, she tripped over something; it was a large wooden box. She grabbed the box and ran into were Jeremiah was. Nearly out of breath, she said, "Jeremiah, you have got to go in there!"

Jeremiah didn't hesitate, he ran into the room. He shouted, "What in the world is that?"

From the other room, Naomi loudly replied, "It's blood."

Jeremiah then went back into were Naomi was and sat next to her. She was still holding onto the large box. Jeremiah then said, "That's a lot of blood. I wonder if Wilton is hurt."

"Well he wasn't hurt before the funeral, because I saw him help carrying the casket to the front of the church. Besides that, the blood is dried up. That blood had been on there for a while," said Naomi.

"Where the hell is he, I need so answers," said Jeremiah.

As Jeremiah continued to talk, Naomi opened the box. Inside the box was pieces of women's jewelry, women's undergarments, and one small white shoe.

"Look, this is all women's stuff," said Naomi.

Jeremiah looked through the things in the box. "I'm not getting this. What in the world is he doing with this type of stuff," asked Jeremiah.

"I know, why would he have these things?" she asked. Then she noticed what appeared to be a necklace similar to the one Lydia had been wearing when she came down from Chicago.

"No!" shouted Naomi.

"What's wrong?" asked Jeremiah.

Naomi began crying and nervously shaking. She pulled the necklace from the box, and said, "This is my baby's necklace. Jeremiah this is Lydia's necklace!"

"Are you sure," asked Jeremiah.

"Are you sure that's Momma Ruth's necklace in your hands?" asked Naomi.

Jeremiah then took the necklace from Naomi's hand, and replied, "Come on, bring the box, and let's go."

Chapter Seventeen

As mysteriously as he had arrived in 1949,
Wilton mysteriously had left.

Shame On You Wilton ...

MANY AMBIGUOUS THOUGHTS FILLED Jeremiah's mind as he and Naomi walked. The coincidences surrounding Wilton were too great to ignore. Once the two finally arrived at their house, they saw that most of the people from the funeral were there. He was particularly glad to see Napoleon Martin and the other out of town people. He wanted them to look through the box to see if they recognized any of the items.

Jeremiah wanted to talk to all the adults about what him and Naomi had discovered. He asked all the small children to go outside while the adults talked. He then placed the large box on the floor and asked for everyone's attention. They all eagerly waited on what he had to tell them.

Once the room calmed down, Jeremiah began to speak, saying, "Everybody, this is a box we got from Wilton's house. I want you to all look at what's inside to see if you recognize anything. Before we do that, I need to ask Harold, Ronnie, and Kent if either of you gave this necklace to Miry?"

The three men carefully looked at the necklace, but they all denied having giving the necklace to Miriam. Harold then spoke up, "Hey Jay, this looks like the same necklace Momma Ruth used to wear all the

118

time. I know because it has her initials carved on it." Both Ronnie and Kent agreed with Harold.

"It is Momma's necklace. What me and Naomi were trying to figure out, is how it ended up in New Hope. Ruby gave it to us at the funeral. She said that Miry had given it to her the very same day she stopped talking," said Jeremiah.

As with Jeremiah and Naomi, everyone was confused about how his mother's necklace ended up in Arkansas at all. Jeremiah proceeded to open the box and show off the things inside. Napoleon and a the people that were with him, began to recognize some of the things as to have belonged to their missing loved ones.

One of the men with Napoleon saw the one small white shoe and grabbed it. He fell to his knees! Crying, he exclaimed, "Jesus no!"

The man tightly held the shoe to his chest while he cried. The people with him also knew that the shoe belonged to his 10 year old daughter. Jeremiah then asked him, "Are you okay?"

The man became visibly livid, and shouted, "No I'm not okay! This is my baby's shoe. She was wearing it the last time we saw her. How in the hell did it end up miles away is this damn box?"

The man's friends tried to calm him, but his anger only grew stronger. Napoleon and the others began to identify the different pieces in the box as belonging to the other girls that disappeared from their town.

By now there were many emotions circulating through the room. Naomi showed the necklace that she had found to Ruth. She immediately identified the necklace as belonging to Lydia. Once she had looked through the undergarments, she identified a piece as belonging to Lydia. Naomi also identified one piece of the undergarments as Miriam's.

By the time that everyone had looked through the things in the box, they all had come to the same conclusion; Wilton was responsible for their loved ones disappearances.

Since Wilton had arrived in New Hope in 1949, there had been five unexplained disappearances. Property belonging to all five of the young girls had just been found in a box retrieved from Wilton's house.

All the new information was especially hard for Jeremiah to accept. His mother had taken Wilton in as her own. He had allowed Wilton to live amongst his family. He had helped Wilton get back on his feet. Jeremiah loved Wilton, but his love for him wasn't going to protect him from answering to his transgressions against the innocent.

All the men in the house went on an intense manhunt for Wilton. They looked well into the night. They continued looking for him for days, but to no avail they didn't find him. As mysteriously as he had arrived in 1949, Wilton mysteriously had left. Wilton left behind great destruction. He was welcomed into a loving community and deceived everyone.

The Ending to a Sad Chapter ...

The Strong's, as well as everyone else in New Hope began to gradually mend their lives back together. Deborah and all who had come with her from Chicago, had returned there. Although Naomi and Jeremiah's remaining children loved them, they did not want to live in New Hope. Sarah returned to Little Rock, while Seth and James moved to Chicago. All of the family that had moved away, stayed in touch with their family left in New Hope.

One evening in 1956, the sky was unusually dark, the sounds of wild animals filled the air. Gertrude had saw to all Jessie's family coming to be by her bedside. Now 85, Jessie wasn't able to fight against her ailments; her body began to shut down.

As usual Naomi was in the room bathing Jessie, and in a frail tone, Jessie asked Naomi, "Where's Jeremiah?"

"He's in the front Granny. Why? I'm sorry, I mean, do you want me to get him for you?" asked Naomi.

"Yes baby. Go get him for me," replied Jessie.

Naomi went into the other room to get Jeremiah, as Jessie had requested. When the two entered the room, Jessie said, "Naomi, can you leave us alone?"

Naomi walked over and kissed Jessie on the lips, while she lovingly stroked Jessie's cheek, and said, "Yes Granny. I'll leave you to alone, but if you need me I'm right on the other side of the door. I love Granny."

"Me to baby," said Jessie.

Jessie motioned for Jeremiah to come sit next to her. He walked over to the bed, and took Jessie's hand and held it in his, and said, "Yes Granny, you wanted me."

As Jessie laid there, thoughts of how she had chose to live her life up to this point, were many. All the guilt and hatred that she had imbedded within her, caused her to cry. Crying is something that no one had ever seen Jessie do. She gripped Jeremiah's hand, and said, "Yes son, I called you in here."

"I'm here Granny," replied Jeremiah.

It too all the strength that she had left in her body to respond to Jeremiah. She motioned for him to come closer, so he would be able to hear her. "Okay Granny, I can hear you now," said Jeremiah.

"If you don't mind let this be between me and you," said Jessie.

"Sure Granny, if that's what you want," said Jeremiah.

Jessie looked at Jeremiah and she began to unburden herself, saying, "I don't want you to think harsh of me because I call you Preacher man. I guess I was a fair bit jealous of how close you were with God. I should have never felt that way. Even though I didn't get that kind of rearing from my momma, I did find God after I met Don. He wasn't always good to me. I prayed and I prayed to God to help me and to save Don. I got tired of waiting, so I took matters into my own hands. That's when I chose to take care of my problems on my own. I see now, in my old age, that doing things my way was not the right way," said Jessie.

Many tears started to fall from Jessie's eyes. Jeremiah reached and got his handkerchief from his back pocket and began wiping the tears from Jessie's face. As Jeremiah was drying her tears, he said, "It's okay Granny, let it out. It's okay to cry."

Jessie put a kind smile on her face and gently stroked the side of Jeremiah's face, and said, "I don't care what anybody does or say to you, you always have a kind word. You and Naomi are so lucky to have each other."

Jessie's demeanor and tone suddenly changed and she said, "Jeremiah, I've hurt a lot of people. I thought I was protecting my girls, and the whole time I was hurting myself. I didn't care who I hurt. Even though my hands didn't touch blood, they still have blood on them."

Jeremiah was stunned over Jessie confessing that she had blood on her hands. In the same breath, he didn't want her to feel judged by him, and he said, "Granny, you know, all of God's children have fallen short of His glory. No one is without sin." "Granny, God sent his only son so that you, me, and all his other children could have life. He knew the things you did in secret, before you even did them. He has always been there, but it is up to us as His servants to choose to fight our own battles, or let him fight them," said Jeremiah.

"I know what you're saying, but the things I've done, are just to awful. I had life taken away. I hurt small children who hadn't done a thing to anybody. God is not going to forgive me for that!" said Jessie.

Relieving her guilt and shame, overwhelmed Jessie. She began to cry uncontrollably. Jeremiah continued to wipe her tears. He then pulled her hand up to his cheek. With tears now flowing from his eyes, Jeremiah said, "Granny, Granny, hush. Stop it! As long as you have breath in your body, it's not too late to be forgiven. God knows you better than you know yourself. He and only he knows your true heart. You don't have to confess your sins to me, cast your sins and your worries unto him. He's here Granny, He's here! He didn't leave you, you left him, but now you're here. Call on His name!"

Jessie's spirit revived and the strength in body was restored! She stopped crying in sorrow and started crying in joy! She began to call on the name of God! With an uplifted shout, she said, "Jesus! Oh my sweet Jesus! I come to you baring a heavy load. I know that you blood was shed for my sins. Jesus! I thank you, I thank you for giving your life for me, a sinner. I don't deserve your forgiveness or your mercy. Through you, I know that I will be forgiven. My God, Father Almighty, your word says that if we confess our sins, you are faithful and just to forgive us our sins and to cleanse us from all unrighteousness! God I'm coming to you through your son, asking for your forgiveness."

Jessie, with a smile on her face, looked up at Jeremiah and said, "I've been forgiven, and I've forgiven myself. Please let my all my children know that I love them and I love you to Preacher man. My time has come." She then smiled, kissed Jeremiah's hand, and took her last breath.

Back in Chicago ...

It was a typical day for Mr. Jones, a corner store owner on the south side of Chicago. He was busy attending to his customers when a stranger approached him.

"Yes sir, can I help you?" asked Mr. Jones.

The man replied, "Yes, I'm new to Chicago and I don't have any family here. I was wondering if you could help me out with a job. I don't care what the job calls for, I just really need to get back on my feet."

Mr. Jones was initially skeptical, and responded, "Well, you are older than anyone I would normally hire, but I'm sure that I can find something for you to do. Oh, I didn't catch your name."

The man tilts his hat and said, "It's Wilton, pleased to meet you."

The End